"Unseen Footsteps of Jesus"

OLAM HABA

(Future World)

Mysteries Book 7-"The Sunset"

JERRY AYERS

authorHOUSE

AuthorHouse™
1663 Liberty Drive
Bloomington, IN 47403
www.authorhouse.com
Phone: 833-262-8899

© *2023 Jerry Ayers. All rights reserved.*

No part of this book may be reproduced, stored in a retrieval system, or transmitted by any means without the written permission of the author.

Published by AuthorHouse 02/10/2023

ISBN: 978-1-7283-7813-8 (sc)
ISBN: 978-1-7283-7811-4 (hc)
ISBN: 978-1-7283-7812-1 (e)

Library of Congress Control Number: 2023901780

Print information available on the last page.

Any people depicted in stock imagery provided by Getty Images are models, and such images are being used for illustrative purposes only.
Certain stock imagery © Getty Images.

This book is printed on acid-free paper.

Because of the dynamic nature of the Internet, any web addresses or links contained in this book may have changed since publication and may no longer be valid. The views expressed in this work are solely those of the author and do not necessarily reflect the views of the publisher, and the publisher hereby disclaims any responsibility for them.

CONTENTS

Chapter 1 1
Chapter 2 11
Chapter 3 22
Chapter 4 30
Chapter 5 43
Chapter 6 53
Chapter 7 63
Chapter 8 73
Chapter 9 83
Chapter 10 94
Chapter 11 104
Chapter 12 114

1

...a continuous roaring earth shaking thunder woke up the slumbering Yowchanan (John) and Yirmyah Aer (Jerry Ayers). Was the Island of Patmos being swallowed up by turbulent waters of the Aegean Sea? Did a volcano just erupt on this desolate island shaking the rocks inside the cave that was now the home of Yowchanan (John) and his two assistants? Yirmyah rose up from his sleeping spot on the hard cool cave dirt floor and went to the side of his long-time aged friend Yowchanan (John) and helped him set up as he was still recovering from the boiling oil scares. Youthful Polycarp was still sound asleep and snoring loudly oblivious of what was happening. Yirmyah asked, "Yowchanan (John) shall I awaken Polycarp?" Yowchanan responded, "No, let him continue to sleep until we find out what is happening."

The roaring thunder continued to get louder as it seemed as if it was getting closer to the cave, rattling the dust on the sidewalls and ceiling of the rocky cave. Yirmyah went to the mouth of the cave to peer outside and the night sky was as clear as can be. Shimmering stars blinked everywhere in the pitch black canvas of the sky. Yirmyah exclaimed to Yowchanan (John), "That is strange! Not a cloud in the sky. That thundering seems to even be shaking the very stars in the sky and heavens." Then the spirit inside the heart of Yowchanan (John) was greatly moved and he commanded, "Quick Yirmyah get ink and paper and record what I am about to tell you! I have a feeling in my spirit that tonight is going to be special and I want the congregations back home to know about it." Thus in 93 A.D. on the

Island of Patmos Yirmyah began to record with ink and paper the book of <u>The Revelation to John</u>.

Through the roaring thunder Yowchanan began, "Title this writing as *Apokalupsis* (Apocalypse) meaning 'to disclose from unveiling'." Then Yirmyah dictated the superscription from Yowchanan written on the outside of the scroll of paper like an address. *"A disclosure of Yahusha, HaMachiach (the Anointed or Messiah) which Yahuah gave to Him to show his slaves things which are necessary to come into being with a brief space of time in haste. He indicated through sending out on a mission His Angel to His slave, Yowchanan (John) who was a witness and testified of the Anointed Messiah of Yahuah and the evidence given of Yahusha the Anointed Messiah, as many as He even saw. Supremely blest is the one reading this writing to know again and those hearing what was said of the prophecy of the Scriptural prediction and guarding from loss and injury and keep an eye upon the things having been written in this document, for the set and proper time is near."*

Yowchanan looked at Yirmyah and said, "I want this letter sent to the seven congregations back home in Asia (Western Turkey): Ephesus, Smyrna, Pergamum, Thyatira, Sardis, Philadelphia and Laodicea. The Romans think that I am insane so I will dictate it in a mystery and a little mixed up so that they will not understand the true message and will see these writings as nonsense and allow me to keep them safely." Yirmyah replied with a grin, "Yes, sir. The Romans have not figured out that you can't outfox an old fox!" Yowchanan (John) let out a little chuckle and began once again his narrative, "*Yowchanan to the seven congregations in Asia (*Western Turkey*) Graciousness to you and peace from the One who was and who is coming. From the perfect Sacred Breath Who is in front of the face of the stately seat throne of him and from Yahusha HaMachiach the trustworthy Martyr, the Firstborn One out of the dead corpses and the First in Power over* *the sovereigns of the whole globe. To the One loving us and having bathed us and washed away our sins by His blood and made us sovereigns and priests to Yahuah His Father. To Him is the glory and the vigor to the ages of the Messianic Period. Halal Yah! (Praise Yahuah) Lo! He comes with the cloud and every eye will gaze at Him with wide-open eyes observing something remarkable even those who pierced Him and all the races of the whole globe will beat their breasts in grief because of Him. Yes. Halal Yah."*

Then all of a sudden the roaring thunder stopped and the shaking of the earth and sky stopped and it was very quiet and still. So still that Yowchanan and Yirmyah could hear each other breathing amidst the snoring of young Polycarp. After a brief moment of silence a commanding whispering still voice filled the cave saying, "I EXIST! I am the *Aleph* and the *Tav* (first and last letters of the Hebrew alphabet) and the *Alpha* and *Omega* (first and last letters of the Greek alphabet). I relate in words as the *HaMachiach* (Anointed or Messiah) of Yahuah. I EXIST as the Present and Who was and Who is coming, the All-Ruling and absolute and universal Sovereign." Then in a blink of an eye the whispering still voice was gone and the cave was dead silent once more. Yirmyah, with his voice quivering asked, "Yowchanan (John) was that Who I think it was? I have not heard the sound of that voice since I was three years old sitting on your lap!" Yowchanan replied, "Yes, I believe it was! Quickly dictate what I am about to say."

Yowchanan continued, *"I, Yowchanan, even your brother and co-participant in the pressure and in the royalty, realm and rule and cheerful endurance of Yahusha, came to be in a cave on the Island of Patmos fifty miles south of the town of Ephesus for the HaMachiach of Yahuah and because of the evidence given of Yahusha. I came to be in the Breath (Spirit) on the Sabbath day belonging to Yahusha…"*

Instantly at the mention of the Name of Yahusha a big voice as of a trumpet shofar with reverberation sounded relating in words, "I EXIST! I am the *Aleph* and the *Tav* (first and last letters of the Hebrew alphabet) and the *Alpha* and *Omega* (first and last letters of the Greek alphabet), the First in time and the Last of time! What you look at with your eyes and hear with your ears write in a roll and dispatch it to the seven congregations of the Yahusha *Knesi'Yah* (Yahusha's Gathered People of Yahuah) in Asia (Western Turkey), in the town of Ephesus, in the town of Smyrna, in the town of Pergamum, in the town of Thyatira, in the town of Sardis, in the town of Philadelphia and in the town of Laodicea. These seven congregations represent the characteristics of the entire body of Yahusha *Knesi'Yah* (Yahusha's Gathered People of Yahuah)."

Yirmyah (Jerry) continued to record what was seen and heard as fast as his handwriting would allow. Then Yowchanan and Yirmyah turned around to look at the voice which spoke to Yowchanan. Having turned around they saw seven lampstands with their oil reserves and seven oil lights on each lampstand made of gold and in the middle of the lampstands stood Yahusha the Messiah having been clothed to the feet and having been girded all around his chest with a large belt made of pure gold. The hairs of His head were white like light as white as wool like snow and His eyes were in the manner of flashing blazes of flames of fire like lightening. His feet wore sandals of like brilliant shining copper as having been refined in a furnace and His voice like the sound of many waters. Yahusha possessed in His right hand seven stars and out of His mouth was projecting a swift double-edged cutlass saber being long and broad, and His face bright as the shining sun with its miraculous power of light.

When Yowchanan and Yirmyah saw Him they fell with their faces to the ground at His feet as if dead corpses and exclaimed in unison, "My Yah and Master!" Yahusha placed His right hand on each of their shoulders first Yowchanan and then Yirmyah and expressed to them, "Do not be frightened! I EXIST! I am the First in time and the Last in time and the Living One and I became a dead corpse and lo, I Exist to the ages of the Messianic Period. Halal Yah. I possess the keys to shut the lock of Hades and of death. Write <u>what things you saw</u> and <u>what things that are</u> and <u>what things are about to come into being after these things</u>. The secret mystery of the seven stars which you saw on My right hand and the seven lamp stands made of gold, the seven stars are the seven messengers carrying the seven messages of the seven congregations and seven lampstands that you saw are the seven congregations."

Yowchanan pointed towards the sleeping youthful Polycarp and instructed Yirmyah with urgency, "Quick, wake Polycarp up. He must be a witness to what you and I are seeing and listen personally to what Yahusha HaMachiach is about to share with us!" Yirmyah quickly ran over to the sleeping Polycarp and began to shake him and commanded, "Polycarp, wake up! Wake up I say! Yahshua HaMachiach is here with us!" Polycarp slowly opened his eyelids not really fully realizing what was happening in his presence. When he fully got his senses about him he also fell upon his face at the sight of Yahusha HaMachiach. Yahusha extended His right hand and placed it upon the shoulder of Polycarp and gently lifted him to a sitting position and said, "Do not be frightened My son."

Then Yahusha HaMachiach continued, "Yirmyah, now that you have written about the 'Things Which You Have Seen', listen carefully and record 'The Things Which Are.' I want to start by addressing the messenger of the *Ephesinos* (Ephesian) congregation since Ephesus is the capital of the Roman Province of Asia (Modern western Turkey). This is also the hometown of Yowchanan making it a perfect place to start My messages." Yirmyah said to Yahusha

HaMachiach, "Master, Ephesus is the commercial, political and religious center for the Roman Empire in all of Asia (modern western Turkey). It ranks with Alexandria in the Roman controlled Egyptian providence and Antioch in the Middle East providence located in Syria. The great temple of Artimis (Diana) who is nothing more than Semiramis, the wife of Nimrod being deified. As you very well know, Nimrod was the great-grandson of Noah. Master Yahusha this is a corrupt city, instead of worshiping You, they worship this false goddess believing that it is the daughter of Zeus and twin sister of Apollo. They turn to her for controlling nature, chastity, childbirth and even worship her as the moon goddess. Timothy is in charge of the church at Ephesus and You know his struggles."

Yahusha HaMachiach replied as Yowchanan and Polycarp listened carefully to His response to Yirmyah, "The things you have said are correct Yirmyah and that is why I want you to write the following, *"These things are expressed by the One holding the seven stars in His right hand, the One living in the middle of the seven lamp stands made of gold. I know your works and your labor that reduces your strength and your cheerful endurance and that you cannot stand worthless and depraved ones. You tested and disciplined those pretending to exist as ambassadors of the Gospel and commissioners of the Anointed Messiah and they are not. You found them as deceitful and wicked liars."*

Yahusha explained further, "You see my sons, this is a warning for those in Ephesus and elsewhere being led astray by Gnosticism. This heresy and false doctrine of Gnosticism is exploding throughout all of Asia Minor (modern Turkey) like a wildfire. This belief teaches that knowledge is superior to virtue or moral goodness and that the non-literal sense of the Holy Writ is correct and can be understood only by a select few. In other words, changing of the word of Yahuah to make it benefit certain religious sects and not necessarily the true written letter of the Scriptures. Gnostic believers also teach that evil in the world precludes or excludes Yahuah as the only Creator. Thus, this teaching makes Satan equal to the Holy Yahuah. Furthermore, Gnosticism teaches that My incarnation is incredible because deity can't unite itself with anything material such as a body. This teaching is known as Docetism, a belief stemming from the worship of Helen (Greek) gods and goddesses and that there is no resurrection of the flesh, a teaching from the Hebrew Sadducee Sect."

"Therefore I also want written, *'You lifted to remove them and possess patience even through My name you have worked hard to fatigue and have not become tired of the evil.'* You see my sons, there are those of Yahusha *Knesi'Yah* (Yahusha's Gathered People of Yahuah) in Ephesus who have not given upon their faith for the account of My name, Yahusha, and continue to profess to be My followers even in the face of secular ridicule and opposition. However, I want this said to them, *'But I Yahusha have this against you. That you sent away your first love. Exercise your memory and recollect from where you have dropped away and driven out of your course to become inefficient and think differently to reconsider to feel compunction and do the first works. If not, I am coming to you and will remove your lamp stand from its place unless you think differently and reconsider to feel moral compunction.'*"

The Messiah expanded upon what He had just said, "There are those in the congregation who have intentionally not accidentally committed this offence against Me. Yowchanan (John) and Yirmyah (Jerry) you remember thirty years ago Saul (Paul) had earlier commended this congregation for its great love for one another and a thriving zest for Me. Now, today, they have lost their zeal or zest also known as their spiritual glow for sharing My Gospel and showing brotherly love for one another. You see this warning is to teach that just knowing correct doctrine, obeying some of the commands and worshiping in the church on the Sabbath are not enough. The church known as the Yahusha *Knesi'Yah* (Yahusha's Gathered People of Yahuah) must have above all other things a heartfelt love for Me and all of My Word. Sincere love for Me results in a single-hearted devotion to Me, purity of life and a love of the truth. If this change in the Yahusha *Knesi'Yah* (Yahusha's Gathered People of Yahuah) does not take place then I, as the Messiah must reject any congregation or church and remove it from the Kingdom of Yahuah if it does not repent of its declining love for and obedience to Me as the Yahusha HaMachiach."

"Yirmyah, also write this to Yahusha *Knesi'Yah* (Yahusha's Gathered People of Yahuah) in Ephesus, *'But this you possess, that you hate the works of the Nikotlites (Nicolaus) which I also hate. The one possessing an ear hear what the Breath (Spirit) relates in words to the congregations. To the one subduing I will give to him to eat of the Tree of Life which is in the middle of the Paradise of Yahuah.'* You see My young Polycarp there is a sect within Yahusha *Knesi'Yah* (Yahusha's Gathered People of Yahuah) of Ephesus that follows Nicolas, the Helen (Greek) proselyte from Antioch that advocates license in matters concerning the conduct of those members of Yahusha *Knesi'Yah* (Yahusha's Gathered People of Yahuah). He encourages free love and promotes a clerical hierarchy. The *Nikotlites* (followers of Nicolaus) affirms as did the teaching of Balaam of long ago, that sexual immorality including homosexuality does not affect one's salvation in the Messiah. Yahuah hates the heresy that teaches you can be saved and at the same time live immoral lives. To hate what Yahuah hates is an essential characteristic of those loyal to Me, HaMachiach (the Anointed or Messiah). A fundamental characteristic of the wicked is that they love darkness, pleasure in sin and immorality. On the other hand, truly born-again persons love righteousness and hate wickedness and are grieved when they see the unrighteous deeds of depraved people. They take no pleasure in the sensual entertainment or the expression of sinful conduct shown so openly in contemporary society."

"I want you to understand that I use the phrase 'to him who overcomes' is taken from military usage and I will use it at the conclusion of all seven letters. You see the mighty cosmic conflict has begun to bring to a climax, between Yahuah Yahusha HaMachiach and My forces of right on one hand and Satan and the Anti-messiah and their cohorts of evil on the other. The persecution of the Yahusha *Knesi'Yah* (Yahusha's Gathered People of Yahuah) is just an opening skirmish and they are soldiers of the Messiah. The conqueror is the follower of the Messiah who by his or her patient endurance, their courageous steadfastness, their loyalty and devotion even unto death, is an imitator of HaMachiach. Just as I suffered a martyr's death, but overcame My enemies and even death itself and now I triumphantly am enthroned in heaven. Therefore, members of Yahusha *Knesi'Yah* (Yahusha's Gathered People of Yahuah) who take up their cross and follow Me as their HaMachiach to a similar martyrdom will also triumph over their enemies, both human and supernatural and will be a victor over death. An overcomer, which comes from the Helen (Greek) word *Nikon*, is one who, by the grace of Yahuah received through faith in HaMachiach, has experienced the new birth and remains constant in victory over sin, the world and Satan. Even though the overcomer is surrounded by great opposition and rebellion, refuses to conform to the world and to any ungodliness within the visible church. They hear and respond to what the Spirit says to the churches, remain faithful to HaMachiach to the very end and accept only the standard of Yahuah revealed in His Holy Word."

Yahusha concluded explaining His first letter, "Overcomers in the churches of Yahuah, and only the overcomers, will eat of the Tree of Life and will not be hurt by the second death. They will receive hidden manna, be given a new name in heaven, will be given authority over the nations, will not have their names removed from the Book of Life but will be honored by Me before Yahuah and the New Jerusalem, will sit with Me on the throne and will be forever the children of Yahuah. The secret of victory for overcomers is My atoning death as HaMachiach, their own faithful testimony about Me as HaMachiach, and their perseverance in love for Me even to death. It is very important to understand that you either overcome sin, the world and Satan or you are overcome by their evil demonic forces resulting in ultimately being thrown into the eternal lake of fire. I want to make it very clear that there is not an intermediate group only two choices. The choices are either become children of Yahuah and heirs to His kingdom or the other choice of being slaves to Satan in the eternal lake of fire, which burns with brimstone and where there is eternal weeping and gnashing of teeth!"

At that moment in time, Yahusha paused speaking and a peaceful silence filled the once dark, damp and chilly rocky cave. Now His presence lit up the cave and His words filled the air with warmth as if there was a burning campfire. Yowchanan (John), Yirmyah (Jerry) and the youthful Polycarp were all awe struck and speechless during this peaceful silence. The words of Yahusha HaMachiach invigorated the aged heart of His cousin Yowchanan and even healed the skin of the aged disciple where the burning oil had singed and blistered his body. Yirmyah was filled with a renewed energy and dedication to the Gospel as he wrote down these important words of Yahusha HaMachiach. The ink of his pen flowed effortlessly onto the once blank parchment as if the finger of Yahuah was writing the words he was hearing and commanded to record by Yahusha. The youthful Polycarp was overcome with emotions of being awe struck and a deepening love for Yahusha. Then the sound...

2

...of the voice of Yahusha HaMachiach (the Anointed or Messiah) once again broke the silence and His words filled the air of the cave like the sound of a well-tuned symphony playing soothing music entrancing it's audience, *"To the messenger of the congregation of Smurna (Smyrna) write, these things are expressed by the First in time and the Last in time. Who became a dead corpse and lived. I know of your works and the pressure and the beggary of indigence but you are abounding with wealth and those speaking vilification against Yahuah expressing in words themselves to exist as Yhuwdiy (Jews) and they are not but a synagogue of Satan."*

Yirmyah requested, "Yahusha HaMachiach, may I share with Polycarp a little history of the city of Smyrna?" Yahusha said, "Go ahead My learned son." So Yiramiah began, "Well you see Polycarp Smyrna is a seaport city about thirty-five miles north of Ephesus. (Today it is modern Izmir). While Rome and Carthage (the capital of the Greek Empire) were disputing the master of the Mediterranean, Smyrna had erected a temple to the goddess Roma in 50 B.C. At this time, a temple with a figure of the deified Julius Caesar had also been erected in the city. Around 25 A.D. another temple with the deified figure of the Emperor Tiberius was built. Thus Smyrna became a center for the worship of the imperial cult, which is worshiping the Roman Emperors as gods. The city worshiped many Roman gods of the state including Janus who was the god of doorways, gates and entrances and the patron of all beginnings. Janus is represented with two heads facing in opposite directions, evidently symbolizing the two faces of a door. The first hour of each day was sacred to him as the patron of all beginnings as were the first day of each month and the month of each year. January is named after this Satanic Roman god and idol."

"Next there is Vesta the supposed daughter of Zeus and goddess of hearth and home and the state of Rome itself. The fire in her temple was never allowed to go out and was tended by the six Vestal Virgins, chosen for their beauty and lineage. They were sworn to thirty years of chastity and were buried alive if they broke their vows. Then there is Penates the god who presided over the material welfare of the Roman family. The worship of this god of the Roman State included the belief of 'lares' and 'penates'. Lares in Roman religion were guardian spirits presiding over the fields and homes and were regarded as their ancestral spirits. The 'lar familiaris was the guardian of the household while the lares compitales presided over the crossroads. The lares praestites were the guardian spirts of the city. 'Lares and penates' is a Roman term applied to one's valued household possessions which links the lares with another group of guardian household gods, the di penates, the guardians of the family larder. Thus the Roman families have to pay from their larder a penance as a form of punishment for sin to restore good fortune to their household."

"In addition Mars is the Roman god of war. He was the son of Zeus, the supreme god and creator of the world and man. Mars had an affair with his sister Venus the goddess of love and beauty. This affair produced a son named Cupid who became the god of love. The month of March is named after Mars this Satanic Roman god. Finally, the city of Smyrna worships Roma the chief goddess of the State of Rome. Roma was the wife of Romulus who according to ancient Roman legend was the first king of Rome. Romulus and his twin brother Remus were the sons of Mars and Rhea Silvia. As infants they were cast into the river Tiber which runs through the center of Rome by Amulius who was the god of sea, water and earthquakes and Rhea's uncle and brother to Zeus. Amulius had overthrown the throne of Zeus. The twins were found and suckled by the she-wolf, then fostered by hill shepherds. In later years, they found their grandfather, Zeus and restored him to this throne after killing Amulius. They decided to found a new city on the spot where the she-wolf had found them. Romulus prophesied that he would be the first king and began building a wall on the site. Remus, ridiculing him leaped over the first stones, and Romulus killed him. Thus the god Romulus became the first king of Rome. The story about Romulus and Remus is just a corrupted story of Cain and Abel. As you can easily see Polycarp these fabricated gods are lies and corrupted stories manufactured from the Holy Writ as a way for people to stray away from the truth and the salvation message of the Gospel of HaMachiach."

Stunned youthful Polycarp exclaimed as he shook his head back and forth, "Master, Yahusha, how can this be? These lies are so far away from Your truth!" Yahusha looked at Polycarp and replied, "This is what I have to say to the church in Smyrna in addition to what I have already said. *'Fear nothing of what things you are about to experience the sensation of pain. Lo! Satan is about to throw some of you into the guarded place of prison in order that you may be tested and you will possess pressure for ten days. Be trustworthy even in the face of death and I will give you the wreath of life of honor for a crown of honor like the public games The one possessing an ear, hear what the Sacred Breath relates in words to the congregations. The one subduing will not at all do wrong or be unjust from out of the second death.'* Brothers it is important that the congregations understand that the second death will be the eternal separation from Yahuah and being cast into the lake of fire for eternity of dreadful torture. However, only the faithful overcomers will escape this damnation of eternal punishment."

Then Yahusha looked at Yirmyah (Jerry) and began another narrative, *"To the messenger of the congregation in Pergamos (Pergamum) write: These things are expressed by He possessing the swift double-edged cutlass saber being long and broad."* Then He explained, "Brothers in Yahuah, I address Pergamum as it is about forty-five miles north of Smyrna. It boasts one of the finest libraries of antiques and was the place where parchment was first used. It had earlier been designated as the capital of the Roman province of Asia by Emperor Augustus. Then a temple was dedicated to the goddess Roma and the Emperor Augustus, who had been active in the promotion of the imperial religion of the state. With this temple and its powerful priesthood, Pergamum became a provincial center of the state religion. .Caesar Augustus had also added the religion of the Egyptian gods to this capital of the newly formed Roman Empire. Thus the Isis cult had its influence on the Roman religion."

Yahusha continued His description of Pergamum, "As you know Isis is the chief female goddess of the Egyptian religion. She was the sister and wife of Osiris and mother of Horus. She was nothing more than a deified Semiramis and Osiris was the deified Nimrod, the great-grandson of Noah. Isis was credited with magical powers to bring the dead back to life. Osiris was the Egyptian god and judge of the dead. He was killed by his brother Set, the Egyptian god of evil. His death was avenged by Isis and Horus his son who defeated Set and established the worship of Osiris throughout Egypt. Horus was the Egyptian god of the sun and day and the falcon was sacred to him. After Pompey had conquered Judea and Syria, then Emperor Augustus allowed the Mithraic cult to be established in the Roman province of Asia. Mithra was the Persian god of light who fought on the side of truth in the eternal struggle between the powers of good and evil, light and darkness, His cult, incorporated into a late form of Zoroastrianism and was very popular in Rome as an alternative to following Me as the Messiah. In Pergamum the Roman Governor had the power of *ius gladii* meaning 'law of the sword' which meant he had power over life and death."

Then Yahusha said sternly, *"I know where you reside permanently where the stately seat throne of Satan is. You use strength to retain My Name and did not reject My moral compunction for the Truth of Yahuah especially reliance upon the Anointed Messiah for salvation even in the days in which Antipas was My trustworthy martyr witness, who was killed alongside you, where Satan lives."* Yahusha paused briefly to give Yirmyah (Jerry) time to record all that He had said. At this moment, Yirmyah turned to youthful Polycarp and whispered, "Satan's throne is a reference to Pergamum's idolatrous worship of Zeus and the imperialistic worship of the Roman Emperor. The great altar of Zeus Sorter was erected on a huge base on the heights eight hundred feet above the city. It was constructed in 240 B.C. and stood forty feet high looking like a great seat carved into the side of the hill. All day it smokes with sacrifices to Zeus. At the base of the seat is carved the Battle of the Giants."

Yowchanan (John) overheard the whispering of Yirmyah and said, "I am not especially concerned about the worship of Zeus as I am interested in the Roman emperors. In my opinion they are the incarnation of Satan himself and not divine as their worshipers presume. This city is the administrative center of all Asia for Caesar worship. Under pain of a slow death, men are required to call Caesar "Lord'. That is why Yahusha just charged Pergamum as the main seat of imperial satanic worship. Now don't misunderstand me, I believe that the worship of Zeus is entirely wrong and also the worship of

Asclepios, the god of medicine, and the city calling itself the 'city of healing'. As you know in Helen (Greek) Asclepios is called *Asclepios Soter* meaning Asclepios the Savior and this false god's emblem is the serpent representing Satan himself. Satan is not HaMachiach (the Anointed or Messiah) but Yahusha is my only Machiach (Messiah/Savior). Yahusha is also the only Machiach (Savior) for Antipas, whom I appointed as bishop of Pergamum. It was just last year in 92 A.D. when Caesar Domitian had him slowly roasted to death inside the brazen bull altar while the population was worshiping Caesar Domitian as a god."

Yahusha replied, "Well said Yowchanan! Now Yirmyah record the following: *"But I possess against you a few things because you possess there those using strength to retain the instruction of Bil'am (Balaam) who taught Balaq (Balak) to throw a snare in the face of the sons of Yisra'Yah (Israel) to eat image sacrifices and to indulge in unlawful sexual sins with harlot whores and either sex. In this way you also possess those using strength to retain the instruction of the Nikolaites (Nicolatians), followers of Nicolaus which thing I hate. Think differently and reconsider to feel moral compunction! But if not I will come to you suddenly without delay and I will make warfare to do battle with them by the cutlass saber being long and broad of My mouth. The one possessing and ear, hear what the Sacred Breath relates in words to the congregations. To the one subduing I will give him to eat from the concealed manna. I will give to him a white stone and on the stone a new name being written which no one knows except the one receiving it."*

Yahusha made a sweeping motion towards His audience of three listeners saying, "Brothers, I despise with all My heart and with all My strength the teaching of Bil'am (Balaam) who hired himself out as a prophet and epitomizes deceit and covetousness. This false prophet sold his religious services to promote personal gain and immorality. Teachers and preachers who lead people into fatal compromise with immorality, worldliness and false ideologies all for the sake of personal advancement or monetary gain are poisonous vipers. They teach that saving faith and a lifestyle of immorality are compatible. This is a rejection of salvation and restored fellowship that I accomplished on the cruel wooden cross of capital punishment. Those who take the holy worship of Yahuah and use it for personal selfish gain, self-forgiveness and self-authority seeking power and personal monetary gain are nothing more than sons of Satan and must be removed from the congregations."

Yahusha continued to explain, "I am opposed to anyone who is involved with idolatry worship to any degree or level. Just as I am opposed to any within My congregations who promote a tolerant attitude towards sin. I promise to wage war against immoral professing members of Yahusha *Knesi'Yah* (Yahusha's Gathered People of Yahuah) if they do not repent. That is why I use the illustration of a 'white stone' for those who repent as it refers to the custom of voting for the acquittal of an accused person instead of a 'black stone' for those who are found guilty. Those who repent and receive a white stone can be assured of an acquittal before Yahuah but those who are overcome with the sin of the world and tolerate immorality will receive a 'black stone' of guilty and become enemies of the Almighty Yahuah."

Young Polycarp acknowledged, "Now I understand Yahusha. Yowchanan (John), Yahusha is referring to what the Hellen (Greeks) call the white *tessera* which was used to grant the recipients of the stone special privileges. Even the Roman great houses issue their clients a *tessera* for identification when they come to get their daily food and money. Winning athletes at the games are given a *tessera* conferring them the right for free entry into all public spectacles. Even great gladiators are given a *tessera* as an admired hero and if they have an illustrious career the letters SP are engraved on it which stands for the Latin *spectatus* meaning 'tested valor'. We as members of Yahusha *Knesi'Yah* (Yahusha's Gathered People of Yahuah) should have 'tested valor' of victory."

Then Yahusha indicated to Yirmyah to begin writing again, "Now I am about to dictate My longest letter to the least important of the seven city congregations. *'To the messenger (Bishop) of the congregation of Thuareira (Thyatira) write: These things the Son of Yahuah related in words. He possessing His eyes as a flashing blaze of fire like lightning and His feet like brilliant shinning copper.'* My eyes of fire are the representation of My hatred against sin and hatred of the tolerance of sinful actions. My judgement is swift, powerful and pure like lightning and can burn to the inner most soul of mankind. My copper feet are a representation of those who are like 'white copper' glowing red hot in a coppersmith's fire. I am stressing that members of Yahusha *Knesi'Yah* (Yahusha's Gathered People of Yahuah) should be red hot on fire taking and sharing My pure 'white' Gospel message of salvation and restored fellowship to others."

Yirmyah (Jerry) stopped writing and said, "Yahusha your illustration is so appropriate because Thuareira (Thyatira) is located thirty-five miles southeast of Pergamum and is noted for its numerous trade guilds and for its wool and dying industry. This city is especially noted for its purple fabric. The trade guilds in this city are known for their communal meals that includes meat sacrificed to idols and an atmosphere of drunken revelry and loose morality. To refuse to be part of such guilds is personal poverty and persecution."

Yahusha looked at Yirmyah and said, "Write! *'I know your works and the love and the service and the moral conviction for the truth of Yahuah especially reliance upon the Anointed Messiah for salvation and your cheerful endurance and your works and the final more than the first. But I have against* you a few things that you permit the woman *Iyzebel* (*Jezebel*), the one calling herself an inspired woman and to teach to cause My slaves to roam from the safety of truth and to indulge in unlawful lust and acts with harlot whores and to eat image sacrifices. I gave her time that she could think differently and reconsider to feel moral compunction of her harlotry, adultery and incest but she did not think differently and reconsider to feel moral compunction. Lo! I am violently throwing her into a sleeping couch and those committing adultery with her into great pressure unless they think differently to reconsider to feel moral compunction over their works. Her children I will kill with death and all the congregation will know that I am the One investigating kidneys, the inmost mind and hearts of feelings and thoughts. I will give to you each according to your works to you."

Young Polycarp exclaimed, "Yowchanan (John), you and Yirmyah were talking about this very thing when you were discussing the Bishop leadership in the congregations of Asia. The Hellen (Greeks) called it *'ten gunaika sou Iezebel'* translated meaning 'your wife Jezebel'. Now we know that the rumors of the wife of the Bishop of Thuareira (Thyatira) were true. His wife does claim to be a fortune teller and promotes the uncontrolled desires of illegal sexual intercourse of fornication." Yowchanan replied, "Every church must heed the warning of Yahusha. Just because the congregation is crowded with people and a hive of energy does not necessarily make it a member of Yahusha *Knesi'Yah* (Yahusha's Gathered People of Yahuah). It is possible for a church to be crowded because its people come to be entertained instead of instructed and to be soothed instead of confronted with the Truth of sin and the offer of salvation. This type of congregation is a highly successful country club rather than a real congregation being members of Yahusha *Knesi'Yah* (Yahusha's Gathered People of Yahuah). All congregations must reject not tolerate all spokespersons who put their own words above the Truth of the Holy Writ revelation and who state that Yahuah accepts within the congregation any who willfully commits acts of immorality and participates in the world's evil pleasures. Even though some in the congregation will often tolerate such false teaching because of indifference, personal friendships or fear of confrontation or because of a desire for peace, harmony, personal advancement or money. Yahuah will destroy such a congregation along with its leaders."

Yahusha nodded in agreement with Yowchanan and then continued, *"But I relate in words and to the remaining ones in Thuaterira (Thyatira) as many as not possessing this teaching and who did not know the profound mystery of Satan as they say, I am throwing on you other things of weight but what you use strength to retain until I will come. The one subduing and the one guarding from injury or loss and keeping an eye upon until the conclusion of My works, I will give him the privilege of delegated influence over the foreign pagan races and he will tend to them as a shepherd with a cane of iron. They are crushed and shattered in the manner of earthen clay vessels. Just as I also have received from my Father and I will give him the Morning Star. He having an ear hear what the Scared Breath relates in words to the congregations."*

Yowchanan looked at Polycarp and asked, "Do you fully understand what Yahusha is saying? There are those in the congregation who hold to the Word of Yahusha and His righteous standards. Yahuah knows them and promises that they will rule with Him over the nations because they did not tolerate sin. The mysteries of Satan are the false doctrines especially the state worship of emperors. We are warned here that participation in such doctrines exposes us to Satan's powers, which leads us to the unconscious and later conscious desire of becoming like Satan himself. The HaMachiach is the bright Morning Star. Yahusha is not referring to the pagan worship of a 'morning star' known as Ishtar, the chief goddess of Babylonia and Assyria. She is also identified as the Roman Venus; Semitic Astarte; Greek Aphrodite and Ashtoreth the wife of Baal the sun and rain god of the Canaanites who was the personification of Satan himself. The true Morning Star leads to life, not death."

3

With four of the seven letters dictated by Yahusha to Yowchanan (John) and recorded by Yirmyah, Yirmyah needed to get another stack of parchment paper. As Yirmyah was getting settled back down, Yahusha nodded in his direction indicating that He was ready to begin again, *"To the messenger of the congregation of Sardeis (Sardis) write: These things expressed in words by He possessing the seven currents of air and the seven stars. I know your works that you possess the Name and that you live and you are dead. By watching and confirm the things remaining which are about to die because I have not found your works being finished in the face of Yahuah. Exercise your memory and recollect accordingly how you received and heard and kept and thought differently to reconsider to feel moral compunction! Certainly, if you do not keep awake and watch I will arrive on you as a thief and you will not at all know what hour I arrive on you. You possess a few names also in Sardeis (Sardis) which do not soil and defile their robes and they walk at large and tread all around with Me in white because they are deserving. He subduing He will be clothed in white clothes and I will not at all erase or smear out to obliterate his name out of the Scroll of Life and I will acknowledge his name in the face of My Father and in the face of His angels. To one possessing an ear, hear what the Sacred Breath related in words to the congregations."*

Yirmyah looked up from his quill pen and parchment and said, "Now Polycarp you need to understand that Sardeis (Sardis) is thirty miles south of Thyatira and is the capital of ancient Lydia. It is a very important city of Asia Minor and was greatly damaged by an earthquake in 17 A.D. However, with the help of the Roman

Emperor Tiberius it made a rapid recovery. The interest of the city in the imperial cult, which was stimulated by the emperor's gracious act, is shown by its competition with Smyrna for the privilege of representing the Asiatic cities by erecting a temple to Emperor Tiberius. The congregation in Sardis is spiritually dead, with only a few of its members remaining faithful to the Gospel. Outwardly the congregation appears alive and has a reputation of success and spirituality. It has an exciting form of worship but not the true power and righteousness of the Sacred Breath. However the eyes of blazing fire of Yahusha can see the inner lives and hearts of the people who were just putting on a show, going through the motions of worship, putting in their social hour of obligation and warming a place on worship days just so everyone could see them in attendance. The congregation has become just like the congregation in Ephesus being lethargic in worship and not walking a daily life of Yahusha HaMachiach (Anointed/Messiah). Yahusha wants them to get back what they once had spiritually by REMEMBER--REPENT--DO!"

Then the elderly Yowchanan chimed in, "You see Polycarp even though the majority of the congregation in Sardis has lost its way, there still remains a very few members of Yahusha *Knesi'Yah* (Yahusha's Gathered People of Yahuah) faithful to HaMachiach (the Anointed/Messiah). Throughout ancient history, even from the beginning of time, there have always been a remnant who have not 'soiled their clothes' and who have sought to return to the simplicity and purity of devotion to Yahuah Yahusha, whom we personally know and see here before us today. Those white garments are a representation of righteousness and immortality and replace the mortal body and constitute the immortal body of the faithful members of Yahusha *Knesi'Yah* (Yahusha's Gathered People of Yahuah). Just as a reference young Polycarp, in the ancient world white robes stood for festivity, victory and purity. It was the tradition of the Persian King, who was the first nation to conquer Sardis, to have his special guests walk with him in the royal garden wearing white robes. To celebrate a great victory the Romans have all the city to dress in white garments. The city celebration would be called *urbs candida* in Latin meaning 'the city in white."

Yowchanan (John) continued, "Yahusha has made it very clear that everyone has a chance to eat from the Tree of Life and everyone's name is written in the Book of Life. Clearly any person who experiences the new birth but later refused to persevere in faith and to overcome, will have his or her name taken out of the Book of Life. Understand to have one's name blotted out of the Book of Life is to lose eternal life in Paradise and to be condemned to the lake of fire in the end of times for eternal torment where there is weeping and gnashing of teeth."

Yowchanan folded his arms across his chest and leaned back against the rocky cave wall. Then Yahshua began to speak once more, *"To the messenger of the congregation in Philadelphia write: These things are related in words by the Sacred One the True One, He possessing the Key of David, the One opening up and not even one closes and He closes and not even one opens up. I know of your works. Lo! I have placed in front of you a door being opened up and not even one is able to close it because you possess a little power and have guarded from loss and injury and kept an eye upon Me, the Anointed Messiah, and did not reject My Name. Lo! I give from out of the synagogue of Satan those calling themselves to exist as Yhuwdiy (Hebrews) and they are not but they lie with an utterance of an untruth and attempt to deceive by falsehood. Lo! I will make them that they will come and will prostrate themselves in front of your feet and they will know that I loved you. Because you guarded from loss and injury and kept an eye upon the Anointed Messiah of My cheerful endurance. I also will keep you out of the hour of the experience of evil adversity being about to come upon all* the habitable world to test those living on the soil of the whole globe. Lo! I am coming without delay and suddenly. Use strength to seize what you possess in order that not even one take your wreath of honor like a crown in the public games. The one subduing I will make him a support post in the Temple of My Yahuah and he will not at all issue out yet I will write on him the name of My Yahuah and the name of the city of My Yahuah the new Yruwshalaim (Jerusalem) which descends down from out of heaven, the eternal abode of Yahuah from My Yahuah and My new Name. The one possessing an ear hear what the Sacred Breath related in words to the congregations."

Yirmyah (Jerry) held his quill pen still and elaborated, "Philadelphia is a newer and lesser city and is located thirty-eight miles southeast of Sardis. It is a missionary city and its name means 'brotherly love'. It too was damaged by the earthquake in 17 A.D. and was aided by Emperor Tiberius. Philadelphia is the wine center for all of Asia. Yowchanan (John) would you like to explain to Polycarp the meaning of this letter to Philadelphia?"

Yowchanan unfolded his arms and leaned slightly forward from the rocky cave wall and looked at young Polycarp stating, "First of all I noticed when Yahusha said that He was the 'True' one He did not use the Hellen (Greek) word *alethes* simply meaning not a lie. He used the word *alethinos* meaning real. Thus Yahusha is the only real Machiach (Anointed/Messiah). This is important Polycarp because having the 'key' means that He is the authority to be the only 'door' or way to salvation and restored fellowship. If you will recollect to memory Polycarp during the teaching from the book of Ysha'Yah (Isaiah) who prophesied in 700 B.C. in his twenty-second chapter and verse twenty-two, *'I will give the opening key of the house and family of David on His shoulder. That He opened wide and no one shuts.'* Then Yowchanan turned his head towards Yahusha and requested, "Yahusha would you explain to us about the 'hour of evil adversity'?"

Yahusha nodded in affirmation and said, "Yes I will. I am not going to hesitate to usher in My Second Coming upon the habitual world and when I do come it will be instantly in a flash. This is My promise. Members of Yahusha *Knesi'Yah* (Yahusha's Gathered People of Yahuah) will be delivered from the tribulation period which will come upon the entire earth. Concerning this time, My Word reveals the following truths about the last years of this age just prior to the establishment of My kingdom on earth. This time will involve the wrath of Yahuah on non-members of Yahusha *Knesi'Yah* (Yahusha's Gathered People of Yahuah). Also included in this time is the wrath of Satan on members of Yahshua *Knesi'Yah* (Yahshua's Gathered People of Yahuah). To those who become members of Yahusha *Knesi'Yah* (Yahusha's Gathered People of Yahuah) during this horrific time will experience hunger, thirst, exposure to elements, great suffering, tears, and will experience indirectly the natural catastrophes of war, famine and death. They will be persecuted, tortured and many will suffer martyrdom. They will undergo the ravages of Satan and demonic forces of evil violence from wicked people and the persecution from anti-messiahs. They will suffer loss of home and will need to flee in fear. It will be an especially disastrous time for those with families and children, so terrible that the tribulation members of Yahusha *Knesi'Yah* (Yahusha's Gathered People of Yahuah) who die will be counted blessed, for they will rest from their labor and will be free from eternal persecution."

Yahusha paused for a moment then continued, "With that being said, I also need to clarify that those who are members of Yahusha *Knesi'Yah* (Yahusha's Gathered People of Yahuah) before that terrible day arrives, Yahuah will keep them from that hour of trial when they will be gathered in the air to Myself at My appearing. Those members of Yahusha *Knesi'Yah* (Yahusha's Gathered People of Yahuah) who hope to escape all these terrible things that are going to come upon the earth will do so only by faithfulness to Me, My Word and by constant vigilance in prayer so that they will not be deceived."

At that moment in time the voice of Yahusha became very stern, "Members of Yahusha *Knesi'Yah* (Yahusha's Gathered People of Yahuah) must not yield their crown to Satan or one of his evil demonic minions. Their crown is their faith of eternal restored fellowship through Me. If they do not yield their faith in Me then they will become a support pillar which means that I will honor them in front of the face of Yahuah and they will be in the presence of His glory for eternity. Therefore, as members of the eternal family of Yahuah they will bear the Holy Name of Yahuah from His city the New Yruwshalaim (Jerusalem) and My new Name which will be Yahuah because We are One."

Then Yahusha gestured towards Yirmyah (Jerry) and began the final letter, "*To the messenger of the congregation of Laodikeia (Laodicea) write: These things are related in words by the Amen, the true and trustworthy Witness, the Chief Commencement of order and time and the original formation of Yahuah. I know your works that you are neither chilly nor boiling hot. I wish that you were chilly or boiling hot. In this way, because you are tepid lukewarm and neither chilly nor boiling hot, I am about to vomit you out of My mouth! Because you say, 'I am abounding in wealth and I have become wealthy and I possess a requirement for nothing'. But you do not know that you are the miserable one and pitiful and a beggar and a pauper and blind and nude. I advise you to purchase from Me gold having been refined by fire in order that you may be wealthy and white clothes in order that you be clothed and your shame and disgrace of your nakedness be made apparent and with a poultice made in the form of round crackers to rub in the oil to besmear your eyes in order that you may see. As many as I love, I admonish and I discipline with punishment to train up and educate a child. Certainly, be zealous and think differently to reconsider to feel moral compunction! Lo! I stand at the door knocking, if anyone hears My voice and opens up the door I will come to him and I will dine at the principle evening meal with him and he with Me. The one subduing I will give to him to sit with Me in My stately seat throne as I have subdued and sat with My Father on His stately seat throne. The one possessing and ear, hear what the Sacred Breath relates in words to the congregations."*

Yirmyah looked up from his quill and parchment to address youthful Polycarp, "Polycarp, as HaMachiach (the Anointed/Messiah) explains this last letter you must keep in mind that Laodicea is located ninety miles due east of Ephesus and forty-five miles southeast of Philadelphia. It is under strict Roman rule and is a very wealthy city." Polycarp quickly asked, "Is the wealth of the city the problem Yahusha?"

Yahusha responded to young Polycarp, "Not entirely Polycarp. You see this type of congregation or member of Yahusha *Knesi'Yah* (Yahusha's Gathered People of Yahuah) has lost the power to make moral and spiritual distinctions. They have lost their glow and enthusiasm for My truth and My very existence in their daily lives has almost ceased to exist. These people are so caught up in the material day to day living that they do not have any regard to their spiritual lives. Now they do not even make an effort to have a relationship with Me. Their faith in Me and our relationship had once been red hot like glowing metal in a forge. Now it has grown to be lukewarm as they have put their feelings for Me on a shelf. The only time they want a relationship with Me and call upon Me from their shelf is when they have a self-serving need from Me. However, at this time they are too busy with their everyday lives or caught up in the rat race of making money that they don't even have time to fit a relationship with Me into their busy schedules. Spiritual obedience and worship have essentially become non-existent."

Yahusha continued explaining, "My words of judgment indicate that lukewarm members of Yahusha *Knesi'Yah* (Yahusha's Gathered People of Yahuah) are like vomit to Me. This type of people will make Me sick to My stomach and they will become like useless undigested waste with their self-indignation. A lukewarm congregation is one that will compromise with the world and resembles its surrounding society. It professes and teaches a relationship with Me yet in reality it is spiritually wretched and pitiful. Professing members of Yahusha *Knesi'Yah* (Yahusha's Gathered People of Yahuah) and congregations must heed My warning about My judgment against being spiritually lukewarm. From the bottom of My heart I sincerely invite those people and congregations to repent and be restored to a place of faith, righteousness, revelation and fellowship. In the midst of a lukewarm church age, I promise to those overcoming and remain valid that I will come to them in blessing and in the power of the Sacred Breath opening a door that no one can shut so that they may glorify My Name and proclaim the everlasting Gospel."

Next Yahusha said, "Even though Laodicea thinks that they have everything and are self-sufficient, without a relationship with Me they have nothing. The three main sources of the wealth of the city being banking, textiles and medicine cannot save them from eternal judgment. Even though this city makes Phrygian, a powdered tablet when mixed with water and smeared on the eyes helps to clear blurred vision, I yearn for them to repent and allow Me to give to them a clear spiritual vision. I am waiting outside the door of their hearts constantly knocking yearning for permission of entrance to give them nearness, sympathy, understanding and love for a lingering intimate and eternal fellowship like sitting at a common table and breaking bread together."

4

As soon as Yahusha had finished explaining the seventh and final letter, instantly in a flash He vanished from the sight of Yowchanan (John), Yirmyah (Jerry) and youthful Polycarp. The cave once again turned cold, damp and dark except for the few glowing red embers of their fire. The three men sat there speechless and nearly breathless in complete silence, stunned, overwhelmed and in bewilderment. Yirmyah sat there with the quill in his hand and his other hand on the parchment as if he had been frozen in time. Young Polycarp broke the silence and asked, "Yowchanan, what just happened? Where did Yahusha go?" Yowchanan replied, "I don't know Polycarp. Have my eyes and ears deceived me?"

All at once a familiar small still voice like a gentle breeze filtering softly through the rustling leaves of an olive tree came from the mouth of the dark, damp and cold mouth of the cave. The heads of the three men inside the dark cave jerked in the direction of the cave opening and their eyes squinted and strained in the darkness to visualize what their ears were hearing. However, nothing could be seen except the dark cave opening and the blackness of the night atmosphere.

The gentle voice of Yahusha commanded, "Yirmyah (Jerry) you have recorded what I have said about <u>The Things Which You Have Seen</u> and <u>The Things Which Are.</u> Now I want you to carefully record <u>The Things Which Shall Take Place After These Things.</u> Since the number seven is My divine number, I will reveal to you three men a series of seven visions. Each of the seven series of visions will contain seven visions each, totaling forty-nine. Polycarp remember that the number forty-nine symbolizes the 'time of the end' just as forty-nine years is the time of the end just before the Year of Jubilee which comes in the fiftieth year. The Year of Jubilee is a time of freedom, restoration and celebration so shall it be at the final end of times. Mankind will once again be free from sin and death while a celebration of shouting for joy with a restored fellowship with My Father for all of eternity."

Polycarp nodded as if he understood and then commented, "Yes, just as the children of Yisra'Yah (Israel) were led from *Mitsrayim* (Egypt) by Mosheh (Moses) to *Har Ciyniy* (Mountain Sinai) for forty-nine days and on day fifty the Ten Commandments were given to Mosheh (Moses). That is why we celebrate *Shavuot* (Giving of the Torah)." Then Yowchanan (John) with excitement spoke up, "Good Polycarp! I also remember it like as if it was yesterday, when after Your resurrection Yahusha You commanded us disciples to be shut up in the Upper Room for forty-nine days and on day fifty as we were beginning to celebrate the *Shavout* (Giving of the Torah) a rushing of the wind and tongues of fire came raining down in the room as You gave us the Sacred Breath thus we were given the 'letter of the law' and the 'spirit of the law' on the same day many centuries apart."

Then the gentle voice of Yahusha said, "Yowchanan (John) my beloved cousin and last living disciple. You shall go into a deep sleep and I will show you through a vision future events of the end of times. Polycarp light the torches so that Yirmyah (Jerry) can record what he hears from Yowchanan and Myself during this vision. No matter what you hear from the lips of Yowchanan do not attempt to wake him up from his deep sleep for he shall be in the spirit safe and sound until the vision is completed. Just like right now, Polycarp and Yirmyah you will not see Myself or any part of the vision. Therefore, listen carefully and record everything that comes from the lips of Yowchanan and the sound of My voice explaining what he has just seen. Do you understand?" Yirmyah and Polycarp nodded in a unison affirmation of understanding and said, "Yes, Master!"

The soft voice of Yahusha faded into the blackness as He said, "Do as I have commanded you and do not fear. I must depart for a short time but I will return soon." Then the darkness of the night was silent once more. Polycarp at once light the four torches and returned them to their makeshift holders in the side walls of the rocky cave. Yirmyah gathered all the parchment and ink that he could find and began to organize his writing area. The aged Yowchanan laid his head back down and stared at the brown rocky ceiling. He watched the spiders on the ceiling scurry back and forth across their white silk webs as their tiny shadows danced against the cool ceiling. Time seemed to linger and the three men remained in complete silence as they waited for the gentle voice of Yahusha HaMachiach (the Anointed/Messiah) to return.

After a while youthful Polycarp began to softly hum a familiar worship tune from the book of *Chabaqquwq* Habakkuk chapter two verses one through three. Then as Polycarp continued to hum Yirmyah (Jerry) began to sing the words with his tender baritone voice:

"'Al mishmereth amad yatsab al matsor tsaphah raah mah dabar bi mah shub al towkechah (On my sentry watch I will stand and set myself on the siege mound and lean forward to peer into the distance for observation to see what He will say against me and what I will return upon my chastisement of correction.)"

"Anah Yahuah amar kathab chazon baar al luach maan ruts qara bow (Yahuah answered me and said write the vision and engrave it on the tablets in order that he may run in a rush who is reading it)"

"Ki od chazon moed puach qets lo kazab im mahah chakah low ki boy abo lo achar (because still the vision is for the set time but it pants puffs of air to the end and does not lie in deceit. Though it hesitates and is reluctant, wait for it. Because surely it will come and it will not procrastinate."

As the humming of Polycarp and the singing of Yirmyah had reached the end of the third refrain for a second time, the weary eyelids of the aged Yowchanan had succumbed to their heaviness and Yowchanan was sound asleep resting peacefully with the soothing music as it filled the cold damp air of the rocky cave. Yirmyah covered up his aged friend with a tattered rag of a blanket the best he could being careful not to awaken the tired and weary disciple as his worn out body slumbered to a much needed rest.

After these things Yowchanan began to speak in his sleep, *"Lo! I see a door having been opened up in Heaven, the eternal abode of Yahuah and the first voice which I had heard in the manner of a reverberating trumpet, the voice of Yahusha is speaking to me relating in words, 'Go up here and I will show you what is necessary to come into being after these things!'* Yirmyah quickly scrambled for the ink and parchment to record what was happening and being said. Yowchanan continued, *"All at once I feel like I have become a current of air and lo, a stately seat throne is lying outstretched in Heaven, the eternal abode of Yahuah and on the stately seat throne One residing and He residing is similar in an inspired appearance of a brick red jasper gem stone and a pale orange Sardis gem stone. A rainbow iris is around the stately seat throne similar in an inspired appearance to a light green emerald diamond gem stone with a hint of blue."*

The cold and damp cave once again grew silent as Yowchanan stopped speaking. Yirmyah and young Polycarp looked at each other stunned in astonishment trying to mentally understand what was just uttered from the lips of Yowchanan (John). Then the gentle and familiar voice of Yahusha filled the cave stating, "The door Yowchanan saw is Me revealing to him the spiritual things of Heaven in his spirit. The outstretched throne that he saw represents My glory as Yahuah. Yowchanan is not the first one that I have shown this throne to. I also showed this same vision to Miykahuw (Micah) as he spoke to King Yhowshaphat and also to the prophet Ysha'Yah (Isaiah) after the death of King Uzziyah (Uzziah). The prophet Ychezqe'l (Ezekiel) during the time of exile also was given the privilege to witness this very same vision."

Yahusha continued to explain the vision of Yowchanan to Yirmyah (Jerry) and Polycarp, "As I sit on the throne as Yahuah the two colors of light that was seen can easily be explained. The clear red crystal jasper with its unbearable brightness represents My sinless purity and the orange Sardis the color of flames of fire represents My avenging wrath and hatred of sin. The beautiful green emerald diamond circular rainbow stands for the promise of My mercy and eternal life as the Father, Son and Spirit are One without beginning or end."

The voice of Yahusha faded and Yowchanan twitched and gave a little moan. Then Yowchanan (John) began speaking in his sleep again, *"Around the stately seat throne I see twenty-four stately seat thrones. On the stately seat thrones I see twenty-four older seniors sitting having been clothed in white clothes and they had on their heads wreath crowns of honor like a prize in public games made of gold. From out of the stately seat throne issues forth the glare of lightning and roaring thunder and voices. The seven lamps of fire are set on fire in the face of the stately seat throne which are the seven Breaths, being the Sacred Breath of Yahuah. In the face of the stately seat throne is a transparent glassy crystal sea similar to ice. In the middle of the stately seat throne and around the stately seat throne four living animals full of eyes in the front and on the backs."*

Youthful Polycarp scratched his head and said, "Master Yahusha, I do not understand what Yowchanan just said in his sleep. What is the meaning of this part of the vision? It is just a jumbled up riddle in my head at the present time." Yirmyah (Jerry) then said, "I agree with Polycarp Master. Even I do not understand this vision." Then Yahusha softly and patiently said, "It is alright My precious children, I will explain it to you. The twenty-four stately seat thrones with twenty-four elders represent My unified church body of Hebrews and Gentiles since the number twelve represents My number for governmental order. For example there were twelve tribes, twelve apostles and so on. By unifying My church body of Hebrews and Gentiles each with twelve as My redeemed heavenly body, it matches the required twenty-four courses of order by the priests for My earthly temple."

Yirmyah and Polycarp nodded their heads in affirmation of understanding as Yahusha continued to explain the vision, "Their white clothes represent that they are My redeemed sinless church cleansed by My blood at the cross. The golden crowns symbolize My authority that I have given to My church on the earth against the schemes of Satan and his evil demonic forces. The roaring thunder, lightning and voices are indications of approaching judgments to be rendered upon those who refuse My mercy and grace and instead choose curses. Of course as Yowchanan uttered in the vision the seven lamps of fire are the seven Breaths which represent the perfect, powerful and purifying Sacred Breath of Yahuah, My Breath. The glassy sea represents My counsels as the Father, the purposes of righteousness and love which is often fathomless yet never obscure and always the same to the peoples, multitudes, nations and tongues. The middle of the throne represents its height and around the throne symbolizes the four quarters of east, west, north and south. The number four symbolizes universality and the dispensation of the Gospel which is extended to all nations under heaven. The living creatures symbolize aspects of My Church on earth namely, undaunted courage, unwearied patience under sufferings, prudence and compassion. Eyes are symbolic of wisdom and knowledge."

Yahusha grew silent for a brief moment and then said, "It will be sunrise in a couple of hours. Therefore, lay down and rest. I will return again sometime after dusk and continue to give Yowchanan a vision of *Olam Haba*, future world." Yahusha knew that excited Yirmyah (Jerry) and youthful Polycarp would not go to sleep and get their much needed rest so He gently touched their faces with His hands and the two companions of Yowchanan (John) fell instantly into a deep and relaxing sleep. Then Yahusha Yahuah departed and the cave once again became cold, damp and dark as the glowing embers of their small fire grew very dim and eventually burned themselves out. What a glorious night to be in the presence of Yahuah Yahusha. Now another day is dawning.

In the very wee hours before the sun peeked its face in the eastern horizon, a couple of birds sat in a small leafy bush just outside the mouth of the dark and damp cave and began chirping. They sang a song of thanksgiving to Yahuah Yahusha their Creator for a new and beautiful day of His provision. Their melodious song awakened Yirmyah (Jerry) who yawned and stretched. Then he sat up and went to the mouth of the cave. As he peered into the east, he could begin to see faint colors beginning to paint the eastern horizon announcing the coming of the mighty ball of fire known as the sun. There was such peace, beauty and a surreal sense of hope as he stood there mesmerized by the love painted upon the early morning sky by the fingers of Yahuah Yahusha.

Yirmyah returned back inside the cave and lit a torch placing it in its holder on the wall of the cave. He walked over quietly to where youthful Polycarp was snoring and mumbling in his slumber. Yirmyah gently reached down and shook Polycarp to wake him up. After many attempts Polycarp finally began to stir and awaken from dreamland. Yirmyah then prodded Polycarp with his foot in his side and said, "Wake up Polycarp! Time to go get water and the daily rations from the Roman soldiers." Polycarp grumbled and finally with much reluctance sat up in protest of leaving dreamland. Yiramiah encouraged, "Now hurry up Polycarp! Get going the sun is already about to rise! Don't be late or we will go hungry today!" The news of missing a meal to young Polycarp was like stabbing him with a dagger. His stomach and food were best friends and the thought of the two being separated was unbearable. Polycarp stood up gathered the water containers and trudged out the mouth of the cave.

After Polycarp was clear of the cave and headed down the rocky path, Yirmyah returned and proceeded to wake up sleeping Yowchanan (John). Yirmyah sat down by his aging master and friend's side and with encouragement said, "Yowchanan! Yowchanan! Yahuah Yahusha has blest us with another beautiful day. Wake up and grasp the blessing He has bestowed upon us." The wrinkled eyelids of aged Yowchanan peeked up a sliver and the corners of his mouth slightly moved upward forming a smile. Yirmyah then said, "Good morning my old friend. What a night!" Yowchanan opened his sleeping eyes fully and sat up leaning against the cold and dusty wall of the cave.

As the two old friends awaited the return of youthful Polycarp with the daily rations from the Roman labor camp and the fresh water from the springs in a ledge of rocks located two miles from the cave, Yowchanan had Yirmyah (Jerry) read what he had written down in regards to the vision Yowchanan uttered. Even though every detail was fresh in the memory banks of Yowchanan, he wanted to make sure that Yirmyah had recorded it in accuracy and in the way it was to be shared with the masses if and when they got off this prison island of Patmos. After Polycarp returned with the supplies, the three friends spent the remaining of the day resting and recollecting the events of the previous night and wondering with excitement what this night's events would reveal. The lazy sun sat in the west and the world turned dark once again. The only light in the cave now was the glowing embers of the small camp fire shedding a trickle of light and provided a small bit of warmth in the cold damp cave. Yowchanan drifted off to sleep and suddenly a gentle breeze entered the mouth of the cave sending a trickle of embers into the air like lightening bugs. Yahusha had arrived and Yowchanan began to utter a vision once again.

"The first living animal is similar to a lion and the second living animal similar to a young bullock and the third living animal possessing the face as a human being and the fourth living animal similar to a flying eagle. The four living animals one by one each one possessing six feathered wings around and from inside being full of eyes. They did not possess recreation or intermission day and night saying, **'Sacred, Sacred, Sacred, Anointed Messiah Yahuah, the All-Ruling and absolute and universal Sovereign the One Who was and is present and is coming.'** *As the living animals give glory and the highest degree of esteem and grateful language to Yahuah as an act of worship to the One sitting on the stately seat throne, to the One living to the ages of the Messianic Period, the twenty-four old seniors fell down in the face of the One sitting on the stately seat throne and they worshiped in*

homage, reverence, and adoration the One living to the ages of the Messianic Period and threw their wreath crowns of honor like a prize at the public games in the face of the stately seat throne as they relate in words, **'You are deserving oh Anointed Messiah to receive the glory and the highest degree of esteem and the miraculous power because You fabricated the original forms of all things and because of Your purpose they exist and were fabricated in their original forms."**

Yowchanan became silent and Yahusha could see the puzzled look on the faces of Yirmyah and youthful Polycarp. Therefore, He smiled and explained, "Yirmyah and Polycarp don't be astonished and confounded. I will clarify the riddle of the parable to you so that you will understand. The four living creatures are symbolic of many different things yet all represent the aspects of Myself. They are even symbolic of the four-fold manner in which I am portrayed in the four gospels."

Yahusha continued, "First the lion is the noblest of all creatures of nature. The Gospel of Matthew has the content as Myself as King, the 'Lion of Yhuwdah' Second, the ox is known to be the strongest among cattle. The Gospel of Mark portrays Me as "Messiah the Servant' Who became a sacrifice for sin. You see a calf or an ox are sacrifice animals. Third, man was created to be the wisest among nature. The Gospel of Luke represents Me as the 'Messiah as the 'Son of Man.' Fourth, the eagle is the swiftest of all birds. The Gospel of John (Yowchanan) links Myself directly to heaven which is symbolized as an eagle."

Yahusha Yahuah explained further, "The six wings are symbolic of two for reverence, two for modesty and two for their celerity in executing My commands. 'Round about with eyes' simply signifies their attention to and knowledge of the state of the world and in general My church and their watchful observance of the designs, wiles, devices and various notions and snares of their spiritual enemies. Just as 'full of eyes within' signify their self-knowledge, their diligent attention to the state of their own hearts and the various workings of their thoughts. The symbolic attitude of worship of the creatures is how mankind should worship Me. They are always looking for the opportunity to give Me worship, praise and adoration. Not just from their physical lips to give Me 'lip service' but in truth from their hearts as well. Again, the twenty-four elders represent My redeemed church. The throwing of the crowns is symbolic of giving the glory and honor of the victory to Me. The victory of a restored fellowship because of My sacrifice on the cross as the Messiah and My resurrection from the tomb gives the victory over eternal punishment where there is weeping and gnashing of the teeth."

Instantly, when Yahusha had finished His explanation Yowchanan began uttering from his aged lips more of the vision, "*On the right side of the One sitting on the stately seat throne, I can see a roll having been written on the inside and on the back, having been sealed closely with seven seals as marks of privacy.*" The body of Yowchanan (John) stirred and he awoke, thus the vison terminated. When he saw Yahusha Yahuah, his eyes filled with tears of joy. Yahusha put His hand on the shoulder of Yowchanan to comfort His younger cousin and favorite disciple. The bond of love between these two was unbreakable.

Yirmyah cleared his throat and said to youthful Polycarp, "Just as a reminder the roll that Yowchanan just saw was not in any way like the loose sheets of papyrus like I am using. Rather it is a long roll with a wooden roller on each end and was held in the left hand being unrolled with the right hand. The side where the grain of fibers ran horizontally is known as the *recto*, which is the easiest to write on. The opposite side, the side where the fiber grains run vertically is called the *verso*. However, in this case where the *recto* and the *verso* were written upon it is called an *opisthograph*. The Messiah can correct me but the seven seals mean that the seven volumes are rolled separately and are wrapped upon each other with each volume sealed."

Yirmyah (Jerry) continued as Polycarp listened intently, "According to ancient Roman Law a Last Will and Testament had to be sealed with seven threads in knots with the seal of seven witnesses in wax on the knot. The Last Will can only be opened if all seven or their legal representatives are present to break their seal. The vision of the roll of Yowchanan is symbolic that this roll of Yahuah is in such secrecy that the number seven represents perfect secrecy and the roll contains His final settlement of the affairs of the universe."

Then Yowchanan cried out, "Yahusha Yahuah, my Master, I saw the Scroll of Redemption!" Yahusha nodded His head in affirmation and then Yowchanan fixed his gaze on Yirmyah and Polycarp and with weeping said to them, "Friends, I saw the Scroll of Redemption!" The overwhelming excitement was too much for the aged apostle to physically handle and he collapsed back into a deep sleep again repeating over and over between sobs of tearful weeping 'I saw the Scroll of Redemption. I saw the Scroll of Redemption. I saw the Roll of ...'"

With Yowchanan resting peacefully once again, Yirmyah and Polycarp stood there in complete silence as if frozen with their mouths gaping wide open and their eyes as big as can be. Then Yirmyah said with a quivering voice tone, "Master, Yahweh duh... uh...uh...us th..th...th...this me...eeeen what I think it does? Yahuah Yahusha patiently smiled and replied, "Yirmyah, what do you think it means?' Yirmyah answered, "You know. The end" Yahusha looked at youthful Polycarp and devoted Yirmyah in a brief moment of complete silence and then responded to them, "Brothers, men of

Yahuah. What you are about to witness and hear from the lips of Yowchanan through the visions that I am going to give him is the last days of the universe as you know it and the beginning of the eternal glorious new Yruwshalaim (Jerusalem) as I sit on the heavenly throne as King of kings and Lord of lords. Listen carefully because what he will see in the vision next will……….."

5

"....amaze you. The graphic details are not meant to cause fear and confusion within the new Redemptive Church but rather a sense of reality to those who refuse My plan of restored fellowship with mankind. For those who choose to follow My enemy Satan and his deceitful schemes of this world, this vision will serve as a stiff warning to turn from their sinful ways, humble themselves and earnestly seek forgiveness through their repenting hearts. It is then and only then that I can restore their fellowship with Me, Yahuah the Father and reunite them for a blissful homecoming of eternal happiness, peace and communion."

Then Yahusha Yahuah bent down and gently touched the lips of aged Yowchanan whom instantly began to recount the vision he was seeing, "*I see a forcible messenger angel heralding as a public crier with a great voice* **'Who is deserving to open up the roll and to loosen the seals of it?'** *Not even one in heaven, the eternal abode of Yahuah, was able nor on the soil of the whole globe, nor down under the soil of the whole globe to open up the roll or to look at it. I, Yowchanan, am sobbing and wailing out loud much because not even one was found deserving to open up and read the roll or look at it. One of the old seniors, a member of the twenty-four, expressed to me,* **'Do not sob and wail out loud! Lo! The Lion being of the tribal branch of Yhuwdah, the Root of David subdued to open up the roll and to loosen the seven seals of it''**

Yowchanan (John) grew silent and Yahusha Yahuah explained to Yirmyah and youthful Polycarp, "My cousin and close friend Yowchanan is sobbing and wailing out loud because the condition of the hearts of mankind are so corrupted with sin that nothing of creation can approach My throne of glory and have knowledge of My secrets. However, it is revealed to him, that I symbolized as the Mighty Lion have the only authority to open the seals of the scroll as the King of Creation Who has the victory over death and Hades. My might is not necessarily My physical strength but My strength comes from the purity of My heart." Then Yahusha Yahuah motioned His hand towards Yowchanan.

Then Yowchanan continued speaking, *"Lo! I see in the middle of the stately seat throne and of the four living animals and among the old seniors, a Lamb standing as having been butchered possessing seven horns and seven eyes, which are the seven Breaths (Spirits), having been sent out on a mission by Yahuah into all the soil of the whole globe. He came and took the roll out of the right hand of the One sitting on the stately seat throne. When He took the roll the four living animals and the twenty-four seniors fell down in the face of the Lamb each one possessing harps and broad shallow cups made of gold full of aromas of fragrance powder which are the prayers of the sacred ones."*

Yahuah Yahusha bent down and gently put His index finger over the lips of Yowchanan and Yowchanan instantly became silent. Yahusha stood up straight, interlocked the fingers on both of His hands, placed them in the middle of His chest and addressed Yirmyah and Polycarp saying, "As I am sure you duly noted, the Greek word that Yowchanan used here was not *amnos* meaning a gentle lamb being slaughtered but it was *arnion* meaning a slaughtered lamb with mighty power. However, Yowchanan did not see a lamb at all. He saw Me presenting Myself on the throne with the attributes of a sacrificed lamb with My innocence and meekness of character, My bloodied body brutalized, and the nail holes in My hands and feet. The seven horns which he did not actually see was just symbolic of Me possessing the perfect power of the Sacred Breath (Holy Spirit) to execute My secrets which is My Omnipotence (all powerful) and the seven eyes are simply symbolic of My perfect and complete knowledge of the secrets, which is My Omniscience (all knowing) ."

Yahusha Yahuah continued to explain, "I did not actually take the scroll but rather began to reveal secrets contained in the scroll. My Redeemed Church doing the actions representative of My characteristics humbled themselves in adoration to Me, the Redeemer of the Church with hearts full of repentance accepting My gift of restored fellowship through the butchered sacrifice on the ruff and brutal wooden cross and the glory of My resurrection of the empty tomb. The harps symbolize thanksgiving and praise and the broad shallow cups of gold full of aromas of fragrant powder are symbolic of the pleasing outpouring of prayers as the sacred ones communicate intimately with Me." Then Yahusha pointed at silent Yowchanan and commanded, "Speak."

The voice of Yowchanan continued relating the vision, *"They sang a new chant relating in words,* **'Deserving are You to receive the roll and to open up the seals of it because You were butchered and we were purchased to Yahuah by Your blood out of every tribal branch and tongue and people and race., and Yahuah made us sovereigns and priests and we will rule over the soil of the whole globe.'** *Now I can see and hear a sound of many messenger angels around the stately seat throne and the living animals and the old seniors and the number of them was myriads of myriads, an uncountable number and thousands of thousands, relating in words with a great voice,* **'Deserving is the Lamb having been butchered to receive the miraculous power and wealth and wisdom and forcefulness and highest degree of esteem and glory and blessing'** *Every original formation and product of created things which is in heaven, the eternal abode of Yahuah and in the soil of the whole globe and down under the soil of the whole globe and the things that are on the sea and all the things in them,*

I can hear relating in words, **'To the One sitting on the stately seat throne and to the Lamb the blessing and the highest degree of esteem and the glory and the forcefulness to the ages of the Messianic Period.'** *The four living animals related in words,* **'Amen!'** *The twenty-four old seniors fell down in homage to do reverence and adoration to the Living One to the ages of the Messianic Period."*

Yahusha outstretched His arm towards prostrated Yowchanan and simply closed His fingers making a closed fist sealing the lips of Yowchanan. With His arm remaining outstretched with a closed fist towards prostrated Yowchanan (John) His eyes focused on Yirmyah (Jerry) and young Polycarp. Then Yahusha asked them, "Did you notice that there were three parts to this new chant that Yowchanan heard and revealed to you? Also, please take note that the Greek word I used here for 'new' is not *neos* meaning new in the sense of point of time but rather the word *kainos* meaning new in point of quality."

Yahuah Yahusha the Sacred Breath continued to expand upon the subject at hand, "In the first part, the Redeemed Church sang about what My work as the Messiah and My sacrificial death accomplished for the Redeemed Church. The word 'purchase' in the new chant is the Greek word *agorazein* meaning to give up everything you own. I gave up everything for restored fellowship of the Redeemed Church including the purchase price being My precious and pure blood for men, women and children over the entire world–past, present and future until My return. You see through My blood of the sacrifice on the cross made only the Redeemed Church as My children bestowing upon them the royalty of son-ship as kings and not just members of My royal court. Their reign is not a political or material lordship but rather the secret of daily victorious living under any circumstances. My sacrificial blood also opened up the veil and gives the right of access to Me as the Almighty Father to all of My children as priests. Those who refuse My blood sacrifice and who deny Me as their Master will be My eternal enemies."

Yirmyah and youthful Polycarp nodded in affirmation of understanding as they reflected upon every word of the vision of Yowchanan that Yirmyah had carefully and perfectly written down on the parchment paper. This brought a loving smile on the face of Yahusha Yahuah as He explained about the new chant further, "In the second part of the new chant, messenger angels which are so numerous that they can't be counted join with the Redeemed Church in singing the new chant about My possessions as the Messiah in all My glory. First, My explosive power that can move any mountain on the earth or any star in the vast universe. Second, My riches as I possess everything with unlimited resources. Third, My wisdom because I know secrets as the Father including solutions to all the problems of life. There is absolutely nothing that I do not know. Fourth, My might/strength meaning My endurance of power because I am the Strong One that can disarm all the powers of evil and overthrow Satan. Fifth, My honor as all creation come to Me in total submission because every knee shall bow and every tongue shall confess that I am Master. Last but not least, sixth which is My blessing. Even though I possess all these things and in their entirety belong only to Me, I do not clutch them with a tight closed fist to Myself as you see Me standing here pointing at Yowchanan but rather I willingly share them with My Redeemed Church who are worthy of such holy blessings."

The voice of Yahuah Yahusha continued to fill the room of the cave as He clarified the meaning of the third part of the new chant, "In the last part of the new chant you heard in the vision that everything ever created by Me as Creator Yahuah whether living or dead joined in the new chant to honor Me as Yahuah the Father and their Creator for all of eternity." When Yahusha had finished this explanation, He extended His fingers once again and opened up His closed fist as He lowered His arm back to His side. Then Yowchanan began once again speaking from his lips the vision he was seeing.

"After these things, I can see four messenger angels standing on the four angles of the whole globe using strength to retain the four winds of the whole globe in order that the wind should not breathe hard a breeze on the soil of the whole globe or on the sea or on every tree. I can see a different angel going up from the rising of the light of the sun in the east possessing a seal to stamp the private mark of the living Yahuah and he screamed like a croaking raven with a great voice to the four angels to whom it was given to them to do wrong against the soil of the whole globe and the sea, relating in words, **'Do not do wrong against the soil of the whole globe or the sea or trees until we can stamp with a private mark the slaves of our Yahuah on their foreheads.'***"*

The vision continued, *"I can hear the number of those having been stamped with the private mark, one hundred and forty-four thousand (144,000) having been stamped with the private mark out of every tribal branch of the sons of Yisra'Yah (Israel). Of the tribal branch of Yhuwdah (Judah) twelve-thousand (12,000) having been sealed with the private mark. Of the tribal branch of R'uwben (Reuben) twelve-thousand (12,000) having been sealed with the private mark. Of the tribal branch of Gad twelve-thousand (12,000) having been sealed with the private mark. Of the tribal branch of Asher twelve-thousand (12,000) having been sealed with the private mark. Of the tribal branch of Naphtaliy twelve-thousand (12,000) having been sealed with the private mark. Of the tribal branch of Mnashsheh twelve-thousand (12,000) having been sealed with the private mark. Of the tribal branch of Shim'own (Simon) twelve-thousand (12,000) having been sealed with the private mark. Of the tribal branch of Leviy twelve-thousand (12,000) having been sealed with the private mark. Of the tribal branch of*

Yissaskar (Issachar) twelve-thousand (12,000) having been sealed with the private mark. Of the tribal branch of Zbuwluwn (Zebulen) twelve-thousand (12,000) having been sealed with the private mark. Of the tribal branch of Yowceph (Joseph) twelve-thousand (12,000) having been sealed with the private mark. Of the tribal branch of Binyamiyn (Benjamin) twelve-thousand (12,000) having been sealed with the private mark."

Then the lips of Yowchanan stopped moving and the sound of the vision ceased. Yirmyah looked up from his ink and papyrus and youthful Polycarp could not take his eyes off the Messiah, Yahusha. Then Yahusha fixed His gaze down towards the resting Yowchanan and commanded in a soft and loving voice, "Awaken My dear old friend. Awaken Yowchanan." Yowchanan opened his eyes wide and looked around the cave to get his bearings and in a slightly creaky and broken voice said, "Yirmyah, why did you not awaken me to let me know that the Master was here?" Yahusha Yahuah quickly responded, "Because the task at hand at that time was to record the vision you were having. Now we will fellowship after I explain the meaning of the vision you just uttered and that was made a permanent record by Yirmyah."

With the nod of His head in the direction of Yirmyah and youthful Polycarp Yahusha Yahuah sat down next to aged Yowchanan and crossed His arms across His chest and began to clarify what Yowchanan had seen in the vision, "First, you two must understand that the number four (4) is symbolic of the created universe or earth. Therefore, the four messenger angels represent a message that I have for the entire earth. As you know the four winds on earth are: Zephyrus, Boreas, Notus and Eurus. Wind is symbolic of pending war or commotion. By not allowing the wind to blow upon the earth is symbolic of a time of calm, peace and tranquility. The mention of sea and land constitute the entire globe in a state of universal calm so still that not even one leaf on a tree would be disturbed to move."

He continued, "Just as the sun rises in the east conquering and breaking the darkness of the night so shall My victorious message be a sign that the darkness of Satan's evil powers will also come to an end through the wind of My tribulation upon the entire earthly creation. The seal of the private mark is the Sacred Breath and the forehead is symbolic of being the conscience of the hearts of My remaining children on the earth."

Yahuah Yahusha the Sacred Breath further elaborated, "The number one-hundred and forty-four thousand (144,000) in itself is a great mystery yet very simple to understand. It is symbolic of the unchangeableness of My truth. You see as I have stated before that the number four (4) represents the created universe while the number three (3) represents Myself. If you add the numbers four and three (4+3=7) you get the number seven which represents perfection. Yet if you take the same two numbers and multiply them (4x3=12), which multiplication is a sign of a major event or rule, then you get the number twelve (12) which is My chosen number for perfect governmental order. If the number twelve (12) is multiplied by itself (12x12=144) the two twelves serves as a witness or eternity (the number two) of governmental rule, which the result is one-hundred and forty-four the symbolic number of My perfect completion of governmental rule. Also if a number is squared or multiplied by itself it is symbolic of freedom for My people."

The lesson of breaking the mystery continued by Yahuah Yahusha the Sacred Breath, "Now let's take the number ten (10) which is symbolic of My commands either as plagues or law. If a number is multiplied by ten (10) then the result is symbolic of time given to a person. If a number is multiplied by one-hundred the resulting number is symbolic of the total time given to a nation. Finally, if a number is multiplied by one-thousand which is My commands to the third power or cubed, which represents Heaven or a permanent place for My people who are free, (10x10x10) then it represents eternal time. Therefore, one-hundred and forty-four (144=12x12) my perfect completion of governmental rule multiplied signaling a major event or rule by one-thousand (10x10x10) resulting in one-hundred and forty-four thousand (144,000) is symbolic of My perfect completion of governmental rule for the eternity of time."

Youthful and inquisitive Polycarp asked, "But Master Yahusha, for what purpose did you select the one-hundred and forty-four thousand (144,000)?" Yahusha Yahuah smiled and replied looking at Yowchanan, "A baby bird breaking out of its cell of a shell chirps for food and a new baby lamb bleats to suckle from the ewe. So does the youth of spiritual righteousness ask of his Master for spiritual nutrition." Then Yahuah Yahusha fixed His gaze upon youthful Polycarp and responded, "At that time I will choose a remnant of people who became believers after My Advent of appearing in the clouds, which the number one-hundred and forty-four thousand (144,000) is symbolic. Their purpose of service to Me is to preach the Good News of the Gospel message during the first half of the tribulation period to come. Even though they will be protected from demonic affliction by the seal of My Sacred Breath in their hearts and thoughts, some will experience physical suffering, death or martyrdom. Also, you will note that I did not mention the tribal branches of Dan or Ephraim because these two tribal branches were guilty of spreading idolatry on many occasions. As for the tribal branch of Dan, its obsession of idolatry will yield the antichrist during the end of times!"

Then Yahusha Yahuah unfolded His arms that were across His

chest and put His right hand upon the shoulder of Yowchanan and questioned, "Old friend it is getting late, do you think these two could round us up something to eat?" Yiramiah put down his writing feather, capped his bottle of ink, and neatly put away the writings of the day inside a lambskin for protection. Youthful Polycarp went to the daily sack of supplies and said, "Master all we have is a few pieces of stale hard *lechem* (bread), some spoiled fruit and a handful of fresh berries that I picked on my way back to the cave this morning."

Then Polycarp bowed his face to the dirt floor of the cave and extending his arms towards Yahuah Yahusha exalting, "Loving Master Yahuah Yahusha we thank You for being the God of provision. You have enriched our spiritual souls through the revelation vision that You have given Yowchanan. May we continue to understand and seek the knowledge of the mystery that You are willing to share with us unworthy examples of mankind. Please forgive us of our short comings and may we earnestly seek Your wise council of the Sacred Breath in walking our daily lives of service to You. I also ask that You bless the meager crumbs of food which we set before You and may it nourish our bodies from the tops of our heads to the soles of our feet. I humbly ask these things in Your precious, innocent and majestic name as You sup with us, Yahuah Yahusha."

When youthful Polycarp sat upright and looked at the serving platter he was filled with the excitement of pure astonishment. The serving platter of stale bread, spoiled fruit and a very small portion of berries had become a platter full of a loaf of golden-brown warm *challah* bread, deep red plums, three massive clusters of green grapes and the small handful of berries had increased to several handfuls of fresh-picked blackberries. The three men and their Master shared the meal, laughed and had a grand time of intimate fellowship. Then....

6

... in an instant the Master Yahusha Yahuah was gone, the cave once again was dark cold and gloomy and silence enveloped the three men as only the miniscule popping of the red glowing embers of the fire could be heard. The three men looked at each other with puzzlement contemplating silently in their hidden thoughts what had just happened. After a period of time of complete silence, aged Yowchanan (John) shared his encouraging thoughts, "Brothers, the feeling of void and being incomplete without the Master is only temporary. Remember I have lived through it the night He was betrayed outside the garden and He was taken away from us apostles. I also experienced it personally as I stood at the foot of the cross with His mother, Miryam, and watched Him breathe His last breath and His lifeless and bloody mutilated body be taken down from that cruel wooden cross of capital punishment. Finally, my heart was torn from my chest as I was a witness on the Mount of Olives when Yahusha was taken up into the clouds to sit on His throne in Heaven as Father Yahuah. It is times such as these that you embellish Him through the presence of the great Comforter, the Sacred Breath, Whom you shall have always. For now the day is complete, so lay down and get some rest for the new day tomorrow. Now let the Sacred Breath surround you with peace and tranquility as you are guided with comforting dreams through the night of dreamland."

Youthful Polycarp and Yirmyah didn't utter a word but rather just nodded with affirmation and took the advice of aged Yowchanan.

Yowchanan (John) quickly fell fast asleep while his two companions tossed and turned under their thin and ragged blankets. However, after a short period of time their eyelids became extremely heavy and they both succumbed to the weariness of sleep. It was not long before youthful Polycarp had engaged into a rhythmic cadence of snoring and snorting as the glowing red embers of the fire burned themselves out into a fine gray ash.

As the brilliant sun arose in the colorfully painted sky in the eastern horizon, the three men imprisoned on that small island taking refuge in a shallow cave began their usual daily routines. Youthful Polycarp would go down to the cool spring below the cave and fetch a clay pot of drinking water and then trek to the drop off location for their meager daily rations of stale bread and damaged fruit. In the meantime Yowchanan (John) and Yirmyah (Jerry) would go over the recorded visions from the previous day to insure the writing's accuracy.

About mid-afternoon, a small gentle breeze entered the damp and obscure cave filling it with a fresh aroma as it chased out the staleness of the scent caused by the dark and damp cave walls that filled the nostrils of the three men. All of a sudden the obscure cave became alive with a brilliant light overpowering the darkness and the pleasant fragrances of frankincense, turmeric and myrrh tantalized the sensory receptors of the nostrils of the three men. Instantly, the familiar sound of the much welcomed voice of Master Yahusha Yahuah could be discerned as the greeting tones of His voice filled the ears of the three cave dwellers saying, "*Shalom, yom tov!* (Peace and good day)."

After extending mutual greetings between the Master Yahuah Yahusha and the three men, Yahusha stated, "Brothers, men of Yahuah, this very day I shall continue to reveal the vision of 'The

Things Which Shall Take Place After These Things' specifically the first three and one-half (3 ½) years of the tribulation period. Now Yowchanan, close your eyes and tell us what you see." The aged Yowchanan obeyed his Master's voice and let his eyelids shut and began to meditate upon Yahusha as his spirit began to be united with the Sacred Breath (Holy Spirit). Yirmyah (Jerry) and youthful Polycarp sat silently watching and listening to the deep relaxing breathing of Yowchanan (John).

Then Yowchanan with his eyes closed lifted his chin as if watching something in front of him and began to reveal the vision he was seeing, *"I see that when the Lamb opened up one of the seals that I heard one of the four living animals, the lion, relating in words as of a sound of roaring thunder, **'Come and see!'** I can see lo, a white horse and the one sitting on it possessing a bow and was given to him a wreath crown of honor like a prize at the public games and he issued out to subdue and in order that he could subdue."* Then Yowchanan grew silent and his chin returned back down to his chest as if he was sleeping once again.

Yahusha Yahuah explained, "What Yowchanan just revealed to you is easy to understand if you have ears to hear. First you must understand that a seal represents My lock on secrecy as Yahuah the Father. At the breaking of each seal, a secret will be revealed, which is My devastating judgments on the world. The first four seals have to do with creation/earth, thus the number of four horses and their riders. The sound of roaring thunder that Yowchanan heard was My voice giving a command. The first horse and rider will attack My loving nature and character. He will deceive many to abandon a loving relationship with Me and replace it with the idolatry of desiring the things of this world. The lion represents Myself as Messiah the King and My heavenly nobility."

Yahuah Yahusha continued explaining the vision of Yowchanan,

"Coming from the first seal was a horse with a white color. The color white represents 'purity' and the horse represents swiftness and speed. The one sitting on the white horse is the Anti-Messiah fraudulently imitating Me and the hearts of some men on the earth will swiftly be hardened and reject Me and My eternal love. The Anti-Messiah carries a bow which used here is the Greek word *pheugo* meaning to 'flee'. You see instead of mankind 'fleeing' from the Anti-Messiah, they will run towards him. The reason for a bow instead of a sword is that a bow is used for attacking from long distances. On the other hand as you know, a sword is used for close fighting. In other words, the rider has a far-reaching effect of the power given to him."

The voice of Yahuah Yahusha grew more forceful as He said, "I do not want you to be led astray. I have given the Anti-Messiah limited authority represented here by a crown. The Greek word used here is *diadema* meaning authority of a royal crown not *stephanos* which means joy and victory. I want to be very clear here. The Anti-Messiah has only one purpose at this point and that is to deceive mankind with his false purity and authority." Yahusha then slowly extended His arm and gently touched the lips of Yowchanan.

Yowchanan once again raised his chin from resting on his chest and with his eyes still closed uttered, *"When He opened up the second seal, I can hear the second living animal, the young bullock, relating in words,* **'Come!'** *Issuing forth is a different horse, fire-like and flame-colored. The one sitting on it was given to him to take peace from the soil of the whole globe and that they butcher and slaughter one another. It was given to him a great war knife."* After the revelation of this secret vision, Yahuah Yahusha simply raised His Own index finger to His Own lips and Yowchanan instantly grew silent and lowered his chin to rest once again on his chest.

Once again Yahuah Yahusha began to explain what the two

men had heard from the lips of Yowchanan, "The second creature represents Myself as a servant and My willing sacrifice on the wooden cross for the payment of the sins of mankind in the form of a young bullock in the vison, which also represents My strength. The color red symbolizes 'avenging wrath' and once again a horse symbolizes 'swiftness and speed'. The second seal attacks the witness (martyrdom) of Me as Prince of Peace. You see only through My sacrifice as the Messiah can anyone find true peace. The second rider is 'war' and is given the authority by Me to take away the peace on the earth. The rider of war will come against the earth in great swift speed and strength and will be given a great sword by Me. That great sword symbolizes 'violent death'. The time of tribulation will be a time of violence, hatred, murder and seemingly an endless great war. Now understand that the rider is an evil spirit that enters the hardened hearts of mankind and does not actually kill mankind but rather incites mankind to war and kill each other."

Yahusha looked back at Yowchanan and simply nodded His head. Yowchanan immediately began talking, *"When He opened up the third seal, I can hear the third living animal, man, relating in words,* **'Come and see!'** *I can see, lo, a horse, black and the one sitting possessing the beam of balance of scales in his hand. I can hear a voice in the middle of the four living animals relating in words,* **'One choinix (khoy-nix) [three pounds] of wheat for a denarius (sixteen cents) or $3.20 per bushel and three choinixes (khoy-nix) [nine pounds] of barley for a denarius (sixteen cents) or $1.12 per bushel! The olive oil and wine do not harm."** Yahusha simply commanded, "Rest" and Yowchanan grew silent, lowered his head and rested peacefully.

Yahuah Yahusha clarified the next section of this vision, "The third creature is symbolic of Myself as the Son of Man having the face of a man and representing My wisdom. The color black represents evil causing a great famine and of course the horse represents the swiftness and speed that evil will come upon the earth. The pair of scales are symbolic of unfair and inflated trade practices. I have set the limit of inflated prices during the time of famine. Notice that the scales have a purchasing power divided by the number eight. The number eight is symbolic of new beginnings and division is representative of danger. Therefore, the world will experience a new famine that has never been experienced before and the times will be filled with extreme danger."

Yahuah Yahusha continued, "Remember in the vision of Yowchanan I said not to harm the olive oil and the wine? The olive oil represents the working of the Sacred Breath (Holy Spirit) and the wine is symbolic of the Gospel message of My blood sacrifice on that wooden cross and My victorious resurrection. However, the grain will suffer such as wheat and barley to make bread. The bread and in this case the wheat and barley before it is made into bread is symbolic of My body, which is the Church. It also will experience famine." Yahusha looked in the direction of youthful Polycarp and Yirmyah and they nodded as if they understood the message. Then Yahuah Yahusha commanded them as He pointed in the direction of Yowchanan, "Listen!"

Yowchanan (John) began to speak once more, *"When He opened up the fourth seal, I can hear the voice of the fourth living animal, the eagle, relating in words,* **'Come and see!'** *I saw, lo, a horse, pale green colored and the one sitting upon it, his name was Death and Hades was in the company with him and was given to them the purpose to kill outright over the fourth of the whole globe with a cutlass saber being long and broad and with a scarcity of food and with death, and by the dangerous animals of the whole globe."*

Yahuah simply held up His hand and Yowchanan became silent as Yahuah Yahusha began to explain the fourth seal, "The fourth living animal mentioned by Yowchanan was that with the face of an eagle which represents My swiftness as the Messiah. The color ashen is symbolic of life without forgiveness and as I have stated previously, the horse represents swiftness and speed of the calamity. Once this seal is broken I have given Death and Hades to claim the souls of one-fourth of the unbelieving population on the earth. The fraction of one-fourth is nothing but symbolic of division, which again means danger. One-fourth of creation on the earth will die by war, starving to death, disease and wild evil beasts." Yahusha said, "Continue with the fifth seal Yowchanan."

Yowchanan immediately began to reveal what he was seeing, *"When He opened up the fifth seal I can see down under the altar the breaths of spirits of those having been killed for the sake of the Anointed Messiah of Yahuah and for the evidence given which they possessed. They screamed and shrieked like a croaking raven out loud with a great voice relating in words,* **'Until when Master, sacred and true, will You not try, condemn and punish and retaliate for vindication our blood from those living on the whole globe?'** *It was given to each one a white dress and it was said to them that they should remain and be refreshed still a little time until should be finished also their co-slaves and their brothers, those being about to be killed outright, in the manner also as they were."* Then Yowchanan grew silent.

Yahusha held both of His arms outstretched and said with great compassion, "What you have just heard are My children covered and protected from judgment by My blood as *HaMachiach* (the Messiah), the Savior. They traded their earthly fleshly bodies for heavenly bodies of pure white light showing the righteousness and holiness of Myself as Yahusha Yahuah because I have forgiven and forgotten their sins. These souls were persecuted and killed because of their steadfastness in My Name. They lived their lives according to My Word against the schemes and temptations of the ways of the fleshly world without wavering. Their cries do not seek personal vengeance but rather concern what the ungodly are doing on the earth against My Truth causing suffering for those remaining believers still left on the earth." After a short pause, Yahuah Yahusha asked, "Yowchanan what do you see now?"

The face of Yowchanan grew tight and with his hands he made fists as he recanted what he was seeing, *"I can see when He opened the sixth seal and lo, a great earthquake of the ground came into being and the sun became black in the manner of mohair and the moon became in the manner as blood and the stars of the sky fell to the whole globe as a fig tree throws off its unripe figs being rocked and agitated sideways with tremors by a great wind. The sky separated as the roll being coiled and wrapped up and every mountain and island were stirred from out of their locations. The sovereigns of the whole globe and the great ones and those abounding with wealth and the colonels commanding a thousand soldiers and the powerful and every slave and every free man concealed themselves in the caverns and in the rocks of the mountains. They expressed to the mountains and to the rocks,* **'Fall on us and conceal us from the face of the One sitting on the stately seat throne and from the violent passion of anger of the Lamb, because the Great Day of His violent passion of anger came and who is able to stand?"** Yahusha prevented Yowchanan from going to the seventh seal and Yowchanan relaxed once again extending his fingers and undoing his clinched fists.

Yahusha looked at Yirmyah and youthful Polycarp and said, "The sixth seal brings about catastrophic events against the unbelievers, the children of Satan because they refuse My free gift of eternal life due to their hard hearts and lusts for worldly desires. Not only will there be a massive physical earthquake but there will also be a shaking up in the economic, financial and governmental systems. The sun will not shine and it will be a time of great mourning. The moon will not give off the light of the sun promising the dawn of a new sun the next morning but rather it will be red with My avenging wrath and nowhere in the thick darkness can the ungodly mankind hide. The fig tree is symbolic of scorn and contempt and the great wind is the Sacred Breath (Holy Spirit). The unripe figs represent the ungodly. Therefore, My Sacred Breath will show the ungodly that they are totally unworthy of My fellowship with them as their Father and will be without My forgiveness and can't escape My avenging wrath because they rejected Me. They will not be hidden from My avenging red eye."

Yahusha continued, "Then My wrath symbolized as the red moon will momentarily disappear and the pitch black sky will split and actually roll up from right to left bringing an unbearable light upon the dark earth. Not only will there be a physical shake up of the terrain of the earth but governments, organized religions and systems setup with false gods symbolized as mountains will be shaken. Also, godless governments, atheistic religions and systems set as believing that there is not a higher power will be shaken. Both types of systems anti-Yahuah and godless will be shaken to their cores. The caves of hiding are symbolic of occupations and the rocks represent titles. Understand that every non-believer regardless of their social or economic status will flee to man-made systems for protection from the wrath of Yahuah Yahusha instead of repenting of their sins and accepting My gift of eternal life. They are fully aware that the Gospel message of the witnesses left on the earth is true, yet they want the systems set up by the anti-messiah to save them. However, their occupations and titles are powerless against My might. They will believe that the end of the world has come but are looking for someone or something that can defeat Me."

Then Yahuah Yahusha said, "It has been a long day for My aged cousin Yowchanan and the sun will be sitting in the west in a couple of hours. Yowchanan awaken!" The aged Yowchanan (John) opened up his eyelids very slowly and squinted through the dim light of the chilly cave air. The concerned Messiah said, "Your meager rations from the Romans are not enough as it is getting late. Behold My wonders!" Instantly, the small fire of a few burning twigs became a warm roaring fire taking the chill off the air of the cold, musty, and damp cave. As Yahusha Yahuah vanished behind the glow of the dancing flames on the opposite wall of the rocky cave a woven reed basket could be seen where Yahusha Yahuah had been standing just moments earlier.

Yowchanan instructed youthful Polycarp to retrieve the woven reed basket to see what Yahusha *HaMachiach* (the Messiah) had so graciously provided. Youthful Polycarp stood up from his sitting position and did as Yowchanan had instructed. As he stood over the woven wicker basket he remarked, "Yowchanan the contents are covered with a white linen cloth." Therefore, young Polycarp picked up the wicker basket and carried it to aged Yowchanan who was sitting with his back leaning against the cave wall. Polycarp sat the woven basket down beside Yowchanan who said, "Before I remove the white linen cloth, let us enter into an attitude of thanksgiving and praise Yahusha for His generous provision."

After a brief thanksgiving prayer to Yahusha, Yowchanan removed the white linen cloth from covering the contents of the woven wicker basket. Inside were large clumps of deep purple seedless grapes, round loaves of warm golden brown bread, lusciously sweet figs with their chewiness of their flesh, smoothness of their skin and crunchiness of their seeds and several handfuls of green olives with their bitter and salty taste. The three men ate until their bellies were full and their appetites were satisfied. Shortly after the bountiful meal…

7

...the sun had lazily set in the western horizon leaving the atmosphere outside the cave entrance pitch black except the small amount of light from the sliver of a partial moon hanging against the backdrop of a blanket of twinkling stars. The eyes of the three men inside the cave soon grew weary, so Yowchanan suggested that they all turn in for the night and receive much needed rest from their task of seeing, hearing and recording the Revelation of Yahuah to be shared for many future generations in order to understand the events of the final days and hours of the 'end of days on the earth'.

Dreamland seemed to pass quickly for the three men as Yirmyah (Jerry) was awakened by the soft cooing of a turtle dove perched just outside the cave entrance on the branch of a large bush. Yirmyah stretched and yawned and then threw off the tethered blanket as he arose and went to the mouth entrance of the cave. As he stood in the entrance getting a breath of fresh air on this forsaken prison island, he noticed the sun in the half-way position in the sky before it reached its double light of noon. That meant that it was somewhere around the third hour (9 a.m.) and that they had slept three hours longer than normal. Yirmyah walked slowly back inside the dimly lit cave and hesitantly woke up his two sleeping companions.

After a short breakfast of devouring the remaining contents of the woven reed wicker basket that had been provided by Yahusha the previous night, Yowchanan noticed something amazing like a miracle. The white linen cloth that had covered the contents of the wicker basket was now neatly folded and laying on the dirt floor of the cave. Yowchanan excitedly exclaimed, "The Master is returning today! Look at the white linen cloth! This is the same sign that Yahusha left in the cave He was buried in!" The reader needs to understand that it is an ancient middle-eastern custom of someone folding their napkin after a meal to indicate that they would soon return. Instantly the damp cave was filled with the warm brilliant light radiating from Yahusha the Messiah. The three men quickly bowed their heads and exclaimed in unison, "Master *Yahuah!*"

Yahuah Yahusha acknowledged their respectful greetings and said, "Dear friend Yowchanan tell your companions what I am showing you in today's revelation." Yowchanan closed his eyes and from his lips uttered, *"When He opened up the seventh seal a hush of silence came into being in Heaven, the eternal abode of Yahuah for about a half-hour. I see the seven angels who stood in front of the face of Yahuah and were given to them seven trumpets."* Yahusha stopped Yowchanan from going any further with the revealing vision.

Master Yahuah explained, "The number seven is the sign of perfection. Therefore, at this time at the breaking of the seal all secrets of the revelation of the 'end of times' will have been revealed. The silence is just a moment of rest just as I rested as the Creator on the seventh day. With seven representing perfection and angels symbolizing messengers then the seven angels symbolize a perfect messenger. These are not seven chief angels mentioned in My Word such as Michael, the war angel; Gabriel, the messenger angel; Raphael, the healing angel; Uriel, the angel of light; Abaddon, the angel of destruction or Phanuel, the angel of peace. A trumpet symbolizes a message of warning or alarm. Thus the seven trumpets symbolize the prefect warning judgment as a decree from My voice. Now listen and record My warnings!"

Instantly, Yowchanan once again began to reveal more of the vision, *"A different angel came and stood on the altar possessing a censer for burning frankincense made of gold, and was given to him many fragrant powders of aroma that he give with the prayers of the sacred ones all on the alter made of gold in front of the face of the stately seat throne. The smoke went up of the aroma of the fragrant powder with the prayers of the sacred ones from out of the hand of the angel in front of the face of Yahuah. The angel took the censer and filled it entirely from the fire of the altar and threw it into the region of the whole globe and bestial tones and roaring thunder and glaring lightning and an earthquake of the ground came into being. The seven angels possessing the seven trumpets prepared themselves in order that they could sound the blast of the trumpets."* Then Yahusha commanded, "Yowchanan. Silence and open your eyes!"

There existed a long pause of silence following the command of Yahusha Yahuah to Yowchanan. Next Yahusha stated, "First, I will explain what Yowchanan just witnessed and what you heard from his lips. I am the golden altar and the incense is the prayers seasoned by the deep utterances and groaning of the Sacred Breath (Holy Spirit). The fire is My avenging judgment for My children who are martyred because of My Name. The peals of thunder, sounds and flashes of lightning and the earthquake represent My manifest presence in My power of the Sacred Breath (Holy Spirit) as I enter the earth to inflict great punishment on the children of Satan. Now I will tell you from My own lips what will happen at the sounding of the trumpet warning judgements."

The three men in the cave listened intently to their Master as He began to prophesy of the warning trumpet judgements that would befall the earth and those upon it. As they stared into His eyes, they could feel the pain and sadness of what had to be done because of the hard hearts of mankind. Yahusha Yahuah announced the calamities,

"The first angel sounded a blast of the trumpet and hail came into being and fire mixed with blood and it was thrown to the whole globe and the third part of the trees were burned to the ground and consumed wholly and all green herbage and vegetation was consumed wholly and burned down to the ground."

Yahusha explained the first calamity warning, "Softball size hail and larger will fall with lightning strikes. The lightning mixed with blood means that the hail and lightning will be killer storms. Notice that one-third of the earth is burned up except the grass and all of it was burned to the ground. This means that livestock will have nothing to graze on. I used the color green in this warning because this color is symbolic of life and mercy. However, My mercy is quickly running out and nothing but death is going to come with the trumpet warnings."

Yahusha Yahuah continued as Yirmyah wrote feverously, *"The second angel sounded a blast of the trumpet and as a great mountain set on fire was thrown into the sea. The third part of the sea became blood and the third part of the created things in the sea died, those possessing breath of spirits. The third part of the sailing vessels were ruined and decayed utterly with rot thoroughly."* He explained, "A great mountain is simply volcanic activity and the blood represents that the volcanic activity is a killer. The seas of the earth are now polluted with the wreckage from destroyed sea vessels and the floating, bloated sea creatures."

The trumpet warnings continued with Yahusha Yahuah, *"The third angel sounded a blast of the trumpet and a great star fell out of the sky like a lamp and it fell onto the third part of the rivers and onto the gushing fountains of water. The name of the star is expressed to be Wormwood, meaning bitter calamity. The third part of the waters came into being the bitterness of wormwood and many human beings died from the waters because they were bitter."* He stopped to explain the meaning, "Several blazing meteors will fall upon the water supply of the earth. Wormwood is symbolic of great and devastating sorrow because many human beings and animals will die of extreme thirst because now the water is unfit to drink."

Yahusha Yahuah sternly said, "Listen carefully to the next trumpet warning." Then He uttered, *"The fourth angel sounded a blast of the trumpet and was inflicted with calamity the third part of the sun and the third part of the moon and the third part of the stars and the day could not show light the third part of it and the night similarly. I saw and heard one angel flying in mid-heaven, the highest point of the sky which the sun occupies at noon where what is done can be seen and heard by all, relating in words with a great voice,* **'Woe! Woe! Woe for those living on the whole globe from the remaining voices of the trumpets of the three angels being about to sound the blast of their trumpets."**

Yahusha, King of kings stated, "Now listen to the meaning of the fourth trumpet warning. The sun, moon and stars simply are symbolic of the light sources during the day and night. Now only six hours of daylight will be available on the earth and then it will be followed by eighteen hours of darkness. Even after the first three calamities on the earth mankind will not repent and turn to Me but their hearts will grow harder and continue to reject Me and look to Satan and the anti-messiah for comfort. The lack of light is symbolic of diminishing righteousness and holiness while darkness of sin and demonic activity is increased by mankind. The warning of the three woes is to warn that the three remaining trumpet warning judgements will produce increased intensity and devastation with the next two trumpets involving terrible demonic forces."

The three companions stared at Yahusha Yahuah standing in their presence shining with righteousness and holiness and full of nothing but love. Yet like twin rivers were two streams of tears slowly and gently cascading down His cheeks. The heaviness of the agony and deep concern filled the air of the cave and seemed to crush down upon them like a heavy grinding millstone. The aged Yowchanan choked back tears and asked, "Master, how can this be?" Yahuah responded, "Because Satan is the father of lies and deception. He only comes to kill, steal and destroy. The remaining mankind is totally consumed with the trappings and lusts of this world such as power, wealth and fame. They believe they are self-sufficient and choose to rely upon their occupations, titles and paychecks instead of repenting of their sins and allowing Me to be their loving eternal Father. It is important to understand that it is not I that brings upon them pain and suffering but rather their own choices bring about the severity of their calamities."

Yahusha Yahuah said, "Yowchanan, My dear cousin and beloved friend, you must reveal the rest of the vison of the trumpet warning judgments. Therefore, tell your companions what I am about to show you." Yowchanan took a deep breath and looked into the eyes of his Master and said, *"The fifth angel sounded a blast of the trumpet and I saw a star having fallen from out of the sky onto the whole globe and was given to it the key to the hole of the prison of the infernal and depthless abyss and he opened up the prison hole of the infernal and depthless abyss and went up a smoke from out of the prison hole as smoke of a great furnace. Darkened was the sun and the air from the smoke of the prison hole. From out of the smoke issued forth grasshoppers to the soil of the globe and was given to them delegated influence as the scorpions with piercing stings on the earth possess delegated influence."*

Yahusha Yahuah said to the puzzled youthful Polycarp, "I shall explain this to you in order that you understand. The abyss is the place of imprisonment for demonic spirits and the smoke from the shaft is their dark spiritual bodies escaping upon the earth. They will be so numerous that their presence will darken the sun and their stench will fill the air of the entire earth. The grasshoppers also known as locusts represent the increase in demonic activity which will be like large swarms of grasshoppers. They were demonic beings not scorpions but their bites will be poisonous. What else do you see Yowchanan?"

Yowchanan answered, *"It was said to them that they should not do wrong against the herbage and vegetation of the soil of the whole globe nor every green thing nor every tree except the human beings who do not possess the seal of the private mark of Yahuah on their foreheads. It was given to them that they should not kill them but that they be tortured for five months. Their torture is as the torture of a scorpion when it stings a human being with a single sting. In those days human beings will seek death and they will not find it. They will set their heart upon and long for death and death will turn away and vanish from them."*

Yowchanan continued, *"The form of the grasshoppers are like horses having been prepared for the bustle of war and on their heads in the manner of wreath crowns of honor like a prize in the public games similar to gold and their faces as the faces of human beings. They possessed hairs similar to the hairs of women and their teeth were in the manner of lions, they possessed chest plates in the manner of iron chest plates. The sound of their wings in the manner of the sound of many chariots of horses running to war. They possess tails similar to scorpions and their stings of poison were in their tails and their delegated influence is to do wrong to human beings for five months."*

Yahuah Yahusha stopped Yowchanan and said, "Let Me explain about the grasshoppers. Once again the grasshoppers are merely demonic spirits which are to only attack and inject their poison into non-believers causing unending torment that can't be escaped. The number five is symbolic of completeness. Therefore, they will continue to attack non-believers until all non-believers have been completely affected. These demonic beings are very aggressive and once a victim is bitten, the bite area becomes swollen and discolored with a purplish to black color. The swelling can be so massive to where it feels like the skin of the body is literally being stretched in two. The non-believers will also experience other symptoms symbolized as stings such as difficulty in breathing, excessive salivation, foaming at the mouth, muscle cramps, high blood pressure, nausea, bloating and signs of congestive heart failure. The endless physical pain inflicted upon the non-believers by the demonic beings will cause man to want to die, even attempting endless ways of suicide, yet they will continue to live in extreme pain, suffering, torment and agony."

He continued, "Now let Me explain about their appearance. Being like horses is symbolic that these demonic beings from the bottomless pit are very swift. The crowns of gold is symbolic that they have My full authority to inflict pain and suffering upon the non-believers. Having faces of men represents that mankind will befriend these demons and not fear them. The long hair simply means that their poison is hidden from mankind and their teeth of lions represents that their only motives are to tear at the flesh of unbelieving mankind. Their breastplates of iron means that no matter what mankind tries to do to the demons, man will be defenseless and can't do any harm to the demonic spirits. The sound of wings is symbolic of once they begin their attack a paralyzing fear and dread will seize the unbelievers while the demonic beings attack when least expected and will strike quickly without remedy."

Then Yahusha Yahuah said of the demonic beings, *"They possess over them a sovereign, the angel of the depthless and infernal abyss, his name in Ibriy (Hebrew) is Abaddown and in the Hellen (Greek) he possesses a name of Apolloun meaning 'Satan the Destroyer.' The first woe of grief has departed. Lo, yet two woes of grief comes after these things."* Yahusha was instantly gone but His voice could still be heard like thunder saying,

"At this time, the anti-messiah will come to full power and Babylon will be established in the great city. The world will be ruled from this evil satanic city with the anti-messiah as the supreme ruler."

Then the cave once again became damp, dark and dreary except for the small flames of red, orange and yellow dancing among the small logs of wood in the campfire. The three companions remained in silence as the only sounds in the cave were the occasional popping of the red embers from the campfire sending into the air tiny red balls of fire like fireworks. Finally, Yirmyah tried to break the silence and spoke up and said, "Yowchanan do you realize that not once have I had to dip my quill pen into the ink? It just continues to record on the papyrus parchment the miracles of this Book of Revelation."

Polycarp took his turn at attempting to break the silence and chimed in, "Yowchanan, why did Yahusha Yahuah depart so quickly without saying good-by? Why are you so silent and in deep thought?" Yowchanan replied, "I am sorry dear brothers, but the last words of Yahusha are so frightening for the unbelievers and a dreadful warning for those believers left on this earth at the end of the first three and one-half years of the Tribulation Period. The last two trumpet judgements according to the Messiah will bring nothing but grief for mankind. Thus the last two woes. Much evil will prevail in the last three and one-half years as the anti-messiah will become the supreme ruler of the world. If you think you have it bad under Roman rule just think what it will be like for those on the earth under the command of Satan and his governmental hierarchy of grotesque demonic powers."

The seriousness of the last revelation from Yahuah Yahusha finally sunk in and Yirmyah (Jerry) and Polycarp understood the physical and spiritual implications for the future Church of the Messiah and the spreading of His Gospel message. The earth and mankind in the future were in dire irreversible danger that had not been seen since the days of Noach (Noah). It was at this moment that Yowchanan (John) the beloved cousin of Yahusha realized that if he was given the vision of the Book of Revelation then there was hope of being freed by the Roman Government and getting off the prison island of Patmos one day to have the privileged task of sharing this warning to the unbelievers of the world.

Then Yowchanan instructed youthful Polycarp to gather more wood for the fire and Yirmyah to piece together a meal from their meager rations. Polycarp soon had gathered enough small pieces of wood to make the fire last through the dark cool night. Yirmyah put together a very small meal of lintel soup which was mostly water and a few damaged fruits. After consuming the evening meal, Yirmyah said to Yowchanan, "Oh, chosen one, my spirit yearns for more of Yahuah Yahusha. No matter how much I try to ignore it, I yearn for Him to be in our presence continually." Then Yirmyah began to hum an old Hebrew song.

Next the three companions began to sing over and over until they laid their heads down to sleep <u>Ke'ayal Ta'arog (As The Deer Longs and Thirsts)</u> "*Ke'ayal ta'arog al afikie mayim al afikie mayim* (As the deer longs and thirsts for running water for running water). *Ke'ayal ta'arog al afikie mayim al afikie mayim* (As the deer longs and thirst for running water for running water). *Ken nafshi ta'arog eleicha Yahuah eleicha Yahuah* (Yes my soul longs and thirsts, for You Yahuah, for You Yahuah). *Ken nafshi ta'arog eleicha Yahuah eleicha Yahuah* (Yes my soul longs and thirsts, for You Yahuah, for You Yahuah).

8

While Yahuah Yahusha was painting a masterpiece early sunrise in the eastern horizon with His artistic creative finger of golden yellows, blazing red oranges and soft light blues, the three companions were just opening their eyes following a restful sleep of dreamland. This morning was greatly different than all the other mornings that they had woken up in that dark and damp cave. A very gratifying and tantalizing aroma was teasing their sense of smell. As they sat up and looked towards the now blazing campfire, they saw Master Yahuah Yahusha cooking breakfast over the fire. He had prepared grilled salmon, *shakshouka* which is poached eggs in a tomato sauce and baked *baba ghanoush* a delicious dish of roasted, mashed eggplant mixed with *tahini* a dip of ground hulled sesame and olive oil topped off with light brown and round *pita* bread to dip in the *baba ghanosh*.

Yahuah Yahusha looked at the three sleepy-eyed companions and softly commanded, "Come! Be nourished and satisfied." Yowchanan, Yirmyah, and youthful Polycarp threw off their tattered blankets and quickly joined Master Yahuah at the warm campfire with its dancing yellow and orange flames. Yowchanan said a short thanksgiving prayer to bless the delectable meal that Yahusha had prepared for them and praised Him for His presence once again. All four ate to their heart's content and enjoyed light conversation mixed with joy and laughing. Master Yahusha recounted the last time He had cooked breakfast for Yowchanan on the seashore following His resurrection prior to His departing to heaven on Mount Olives. Yowchanan shared how frustrated Kepha (Peter), the big fisherman, was at the time when Yahusha kept asking Kepha (Peter) if he loved Him.

Then Yahusha Yahuah remained seated and said, "Before the vison of My Revelation can continue, I must make sure that you understand that at the end of the vision from yesterday that the first three and one-half years of the Tribulation Period has passed. Do all of you understand this?" The three companions nodded their bearded heads in affirmation their understanding. Yahusha Yahuah continued, "Good! Now I must introduce the last three and one-half years of the Tribulation Period which is a continuation of 'The Things Which Shall Take Place After These Things'. Just as a reminder at this time of the ending of the first three and one-half years the anti-messiah will have come into full power establishing Babylon and ruling the world as the supreme ruler as he continues to deceive the hard hearts of mankind." Next, Yahusha lifted His right index finger to His right ear and said, "Now listen to what shall take place just before the last three and one-half years of the Tribulation Period." Yirmyah quickly grabbed his quill pen and parchment paper as Yahusha began the introduction to the last three and one-half years of the Tribulation Period.

He said, *"A great supernatural indication was gazed at with wide open eyes in Heaven, the eternal abode of Yahuah, a woman having been clothed with the sun and the moon down under her feet and on her head a wreath crown of honor like a prize in the public games of twelve stars and possessing a child in her matrix cavity. She shrieked and screamed like a croaking raven experiencing the pains of birth and being tortured to produce her fruit."*

Yahuah Yahusha stopped to explain, "The woman is symbolic of My Church and the sun and moon represent time. Since time is under her feet this is symbolic at over time My Church will be victorious as represented as the crown of honor. The twelve stars represent My Church being once again united and complete just as the nation of Yisra'Yah (Israel) once was united as one nation with twelve different tribes. The child in her matrix is My Gospel message of salvation carried by My Church having to be shared in secrecy but screaming to be shared openly with the lost souls on the earth."

The introduction continued from the lips of Yahusha Yahuah, *"Also, was gazed at with wide open eyes a different supernatural indication in Heaven, the eternal abode of Yahuah, and lo, a great red fabulous dragon serpent possessing seven heads and ten horns and on his heads seven diadem crowns for royalty and his tail swept in its trail the third part of the stars of the sky and threw them to the soil of the globe. The dragon serpent stood in front of the woman being about to produce her fruit in order that when she produces her fruit, he may devour down her child."*

He instructed, "Now listen to the meaning. The great red dragon is none other than My enemy from the conception of time, the Devil, Satan. The color red is symbolic of his destruction and thirst for the blood of My Church. The seven heads, ten horns and seven crowns together represent even though Satan is one evil being, his power is diverse and operates in a variety of his evil demonic powers. The seven heads specifically represent seven kings/heads of governments while the number seven represents 'perfection'. Thus the ruling government of the world inflicts perfect terror upon My Church. The ten horns are explained in this way. A horn is symbolic of power. Therefore, the ten horns are a division of ten forms of power given to the ruling government of the world by Satan. Finally, the seven crowns are symbolic of the ruling authority that Satan possesses."

Yahuah continued, "As for the tail of the great dragon sweeping a third part of the stars, the tail simply represents following or followers. The third part of the stars are symbolic of the messenger angels who rebelled against Me in Heaven and chose to follow in the rebellion of Satan and were cast to the earth with him in the form of an army of demonic spirits and powers. These demonic powers persecute and seduce the ministers and teachers of My Church attempting to crush and destroy My Gospel message of salvation."

The Master added to the introduction, *"She produced a Son, a male who is about to tread as the Shepherd of all the races with an iron cane. Her child was seized to Yahuah and to His stately seat throne. The woman ran away and vanished into the lonesome wasteland where she possessed a spot having been prepared from Yahuah that there she might strengthen and fatten her for one thousand and two hundred and sixty days (1,260=3 ½ years)"*

Then Yahusha stopped and explained, "The Son represents Me as *HaMachiach* (The Messiah or The Anointed) and more specifically here as My Sacred Breath (Holy Spirit) as the Shepherd of My Church who will feed My flock of not only My People, the *Yhuwdiy* (Hebrews) but all nations as My inheritance. As far as the child being seized to Heaven, this is symbolic of even though the evil one may make My True Church weak, oppressed and persecuted, her faith is beyond the reach of Satan and hidden safe within My Sacred Breath (Holy Spirit). The twelve hundred and sixty days is a period corresponding in length to the forty-two months during which coming witnesses will prophesy against the predominant evil prevailing in the world."

The gentle voice of the Messiah Yahuah grew very stern as He continued with the introduction of the last three and one-half years of the Tribulation Period saying, *"War came into being in Heaven, the eternal abode of Yahuah, Miykak'Yah (Michael) and his angels engaged in warfare to do battle against the dragon serpent. The dragon serpent battled and his angels and they did not have enough force and there was not a place found of them still in Heaven, the eternal abode of Yahuah. The great dragon serpent was thrown out, the original and primeval sly and cunning snake called Devil the slanderer and Satan the accuser, the one deceiving and causing to roam from the safety of truth the whole habitual world, was thrown onto the soil of the globe and his angels with him were thrown. I heard a great voice relating in words in Heaven, the eternal abode of Yahuah,* **'Now has come into being the salvation and the miraculous power and the royalty, realm and rule of our Yahuah and the delegated influence of His Anointed Messiah because is thrown down the plaintiff accuser charging complaints of law against us, the one charging them with some offences in front of the face of our Yahuah day and night. They subdued him because of the blood of the Lamb and because of the Anointed Messiah their witness to give judicial evidence. They did not love their breath of spirit even until death. Therefore, rejoice Heaven, the eternal abode of Yahuah and those in their tents of protection and communion. Woe for those residing permanently on the soil of the globe and the sea because Satan has descended down to you possessing great breathing hard passion of anger, knowing he possesses a little time that has been set."**

Yahuah Yahusha paused and took a deep breath stating, "Let Me take a moment to explain its meaning. Everything here is self-explanatory except I want to make it very clear that at this point in time, I will refuse Satan and his minion liar's access to My throne to accuse the brethren in an attempt to deceive. There will be a great spiritual battle in the spiritual realm and the Devil and his demonic followers will be confined to the earth. Heaven, My eternal abode will rejoice in jubilation because his evil will no longer be allowed in their presence and at the same time they warn the earth of Satan's avenging wrath and evil destruction. Since the two main activities of Satan are to deceive and accuse the brethren, the defense of My Church is to bank on the merits of My death and resurrection, to be active in witnessing and to be willing to make any sacrifice including death as a martyr."

Yahusha added to the introduction, *"When the dragon serpent saw that he was thrown onto the soil of the globe, he pursued to persecute the woman who produced the male. The woman was given two feathered wings of the great eagle that she may fly into the lonesome wasteland to her spot, where she is nourished there a time and times and half a time (3 ½) from the face of the sly and cunning snake. The sly and cunning snake threw after the woman out of his mouth a river of running water in order that he might overwhelm her with the river"*

Yahuah Yahusha shed some light, "The great eagle represents Myself and the two wings are symbolic of the two great witnesses to come to aid My Church. The river of flood describes the uprising of a people's ill-will expressed by popular movements. My Church that cannot be destroyed by positive persecution, through an infuriated populace stirred against it attempts to sweep it away by a hostile public opinion."

Yahuah finished this part of the introduction, *"The soil of the globe aided and relieved the woman and the soil of the globe opened up its mouth and gulped down entirely the running water river which was thrown by the dragon serpent from out of his mouth. The dragon serpent was provoked and became exasperated and enraged over the woman and departed to make warfare with the remaining ones of her seed, those keeping the authoritative injunctions of Yahuah and possessing the judicial evidence given of Yahusha."*

He explained, "I will raise up an earthly power to protect My Church against further persecution. You must understand that no movement hostile to truth can permanently succeed: the eternal laws of truth and right are ultimately found stronger than all the half-truths, whole falsehoods, and selfishness which give force to such movements. In a mysterious way, every devil-born flood of opinion, or violence, or sentiment, will sink beneath the surface; they rise like a river, they are tasted, and then rejected."

Then Yahusha said, "The second part of the introduction to

the last three and one-half years of the Tribulation period foretells about the one-hundred and forty-four thousand (144,000) Yhuwdiy (Jews), the preaching of the Gospel during the last three and one-half years, a stern warning about beast worship and the foretelling about the Battle of Armageddon. Yowchanan I will show you the vision and you tell Yirmyah and Polycarp what you see. Yirmyah (Jerry) be prepared to jot down the vision Yowchanan is about to reveal." Yirmyah quickly got his quill pen and parchment paper ready to go.

After a few moments of deathly silence, Yowchanan (John) began to share the vision from Yahusha Yahuah, *"I see and lo, the Lamb standing on the Mount Tsiyown (Mount of Olives) and with Him one hundred and forty-four thousand (144,000) possessing the name of His Father having been written on their foreheads. I heard a sound out of Heaven, the eternal abode of Yahuah in the manner of many running waters and in the manner of a great sound of roaring thunder. I heard a sound of harpists playing on their harps."*

At this time Yahuah Yahusha stopped Yowchanan in order that the vision could be explained, "I am the Lamb of Yahuah, the Savior, and I stand with the Gospel Church here represented as Mount Tsiyown (Mount of Olives). The blood of the saints have found their victory as faithful soldiers and servants of My Gospel message. The number of one hundred and forty-four thousand (144,000) represents the full growth of the choice ones of Yahuah, the true Yisra'Yah (Israel) of Me. My Name on their foreheads signifies that they can openly be recognized as My children and they will make a bold and open profession of their faith by keeping themselves as clean from the wicked abominations and schemes of the followers of the anti-messiah. I will be standing midst the Church in all her troubles during the darkest times so that she is not consumed by the demonic lures of the flesh. Their foreheads represent their thoughts and their actions. The harp is symbolic of spiritual healing."

Yahuah Yahusha said, "Yowchanan, now what to you see?" Yowchanan uttered, *"They sang in the manner of a new song in front of the face of the stately seat throne and in front of the four living animals and the old seniors. Not even one could learn the song except the one hundred and forty-four thousand, those being redeemed from the soil of the whole globe. Those are who were not defiled with women for they are virgins. Those are those united on the road to be in the same manner with to accompany the Lamb as disciples wherever He may go. Those were redeemed from human beings, first fruit to Yahuah and to the Lamb. In their mouths was not found tricks. They are without blemish."*

Yahuah Yahusha interrupted Yowchanan saying, "Just a minute Yowchanan, let Me explain for youthful Polycarp and Yirmyah. The full growth of the Church represented by the one hundred and forty-four thousand (144,000) refused to compromise My Gospel message with worldly standards or tolerate immoral and ungodly behaviors. The mature Church will stand before My throne and sing this heavenly song because their spirits have not been dulled by earthly desires. Amid the world-noises of the Babylon to come men of the earth will neither be able to hear or sing aright My song but only those redeemed by Me, those purchased from the earth, can come with singing unto *Mount Tsiyown* (Mount of Olives). This new song here will be in celebration of the complete redemption of the Church and is the song to be sung in view of its final triumph over all its foes."

He continued, "A great truth is taught here. To appreciate fully the songs of the Mount of Olives; to understand the language of praise; to enter into the spirit of the truths which pertain to redemption; one must himself have been redeemed by My blood. He must have known what it is to be a sinner under the condemnation of a holy law; he must have known what it is to be in danger of eternal death; he must have experienced the joys of pardon, or he can never understand, in its true import, the language used by the redeemed. He who is saved from peril; he who is rescued from long captivity; he who is recovered from dangerous illness; he who presses to his bosom a beloved child just rescued from a watery grave, will have an appreciation of the language of joy and triumph which he can never understand who has not been placed in such circumstances: but of all the joy ever experienced in the universe, that must be the most sublime and transporting, which will be experienced when the redeemed shall stand on the Mount of Olives above, and shall realize that they are eternally saved."

Yahuah Yahusha then motioned for Yowchanan to continue with the introduction to the last three and one-half (3½) years of the Tribulation Period, *"I see a different angel flying in mid-heaven the highest point in the sky which the sun occupies at noon where what is done can be seen and heard by all possessing the perpetual good message of the Gospel to announce the good news of the Gospel to those living on the whole globe even every race and tribal branch and language and people, relating in words in a great voice,* **'Fear Yahuah and give to Him glory because the hour of His justice and divine law has come. Prostrate yourselves in homage to do reverence and adoration to Him having made the sky and the soil of the globe and the sea and the gushing fountains of waters."**

Yowchanan (John) halted the great vision as Yahusha explained what he had just seen, "In view of the world the gospel is proclaimed; this is the good news that I, Yahuah, loves the world, have redeemed mankind and that they belong to Me. This word of Yahuah is the sword of the Spirit, and the weapon (not carnal) which the Church uses against her foes. It is represented as in the hand of an angel rising in view of all nations. This is the first of three messenger angels in the vison of the introduction to the Tribulation Period. The messenger angel that Yowchanan just saw was making this last proclamation of the Gospel on the earth. These words declare what ought to be the effect of the gospel. Those to whom it is preached are sitting inactive on the earth. They must be roused to fear Me and give Me glory. They must not fear the powers of evil, the wild beasts, or be afraid of their terror. They must realize that there is an hour of judgment at hand, which will discriminate between the worshippers of the world and of Me, Yahuah. Let them learn to worship the Creator of all, and to turn from the worship of lesser and lower forms of Satanic worship through idols, the anti-messiah and the coming beast. The next two messenger angels speak of the fall of Babylon, the harlot and the judgment on the beast worshippers."

Yahuah Yahusha continued as He outstretched both of His arms, "You must understand that in the final years, days, and hours mankind can no longer just sit on the fence. He must choose between Me and a life of a blessing of eternal peace or Satan, My enemy, and the curse of eternal punishment. My Gospel message is a message of love and forgiveness instead of worldly lies controlled by Satan's demonic kingdom." Then……….

9

......Yahusha Yahuah slowly walked over to Yowchanan and very gently put His hand on the aged and frail shoulder of His beloved cousin. Instantly Yowchanan once again began to reveal the vision, *"A different angel followed relating in words,* **"Fallen, the great city Babel (Babylon) fell because of the wine of the breathing hard passion of anger of her harlotry, adultery and incest that she made all races drink'** *A third angel followed them relating in words in a great voice,* **"If anyone prostrates themselves in homage to do reverence and adoration to the dangerous animal and the likeness of it and receives the stamp of servitude of an etched statue on his forehead or on his hand, even he will drink of the wine of the breathing hard passion of anger of Yahuah having been mingled undiluted in His drinking vessel of violent passion for punishment and will be tortured by fire and flashing sulfur with its smell of rotten eggs in front of the face of sacred angels and in front of the face of the Lamb. The smoke of their torture goes up to the ages of the Messianic Period and will not possess intermission or recreation day and night, those prostrating themselves in homage to do reverence and adoration to the dangerous animal and the likeness of it even if anyone receives the mark of its name."**

Then Yahuah expounded, "The second angel follows on the first: proclaiming the doom of the world-city, the metropolis of the empire of the Satanic world-power which follows the proclamation of the gospel. Destroyed will be the advancement of the anti-messiah kingdom, the demonic hierarchy seated there being enriched with human traditions. Babylon, being arrogant, proud, and oppressive will experience a mighty fall. This third angel naturally follows the other two, which describe the powers which are in conflict: the word of Yahuah, and the Babylon of the world yet the Gospel will triumph; The commission of this angel reaches further than that of the preceding; it extends not only to the capital city, not only to the principal agents and promoters of idolatry, but to all the subjects of the beast, whom it consigns over to everlasting punishment. If any man worship the beast—that is, embrace and profess the religion of the beast; will be burned with fire and brimstone. I am implying that the sufferings of the wicked will be eternal. Whosoever receives the mark of his demonic name, such worshippers will receive the punishment which other idolaters and sinners do. No exception will be made in favor of an idolater, though he worships idols under the forms of an abused and false gospel and none will be made in favor of a sinner because he practiced iniquity under the garb of religion, man-made theology or self-serving deceiving doctrines."

As soon as Yahusha had finished this explanation, Yowchanan clearly stated, *"Here is the cheerful and hopeful endurance of the sacred ones. Here are those guarding from loss and injury and keeping an eye upon the authoritative injunctions of Yahuah and the moral conviction for the truth of Yahuah especially reliance upon Yahusha the Anointed Messiah for salvation. I heard a voice from out of Heaven, the eternal abode of Yahuah relating in words to me,* **'Write. Supremely blest are the dead corpses, those in Yahuah dying from now. Yes, says the Sacred Breath (Holy Spirit) that they will be exempt and refresh from their work which reduces their strength and their works will accompany them.'** *I saw and lo, a cloud, white and on the cloud One sitting similar to the Son of Man possessing on His head a wreath crown of honor like a prize in the public games, made of gold and in His hand a rapid gathering hook for harvesting."*

Youthful Polycarp gazed at Yahuah Yahusha with a puzzled look and asked, "What is this meaning? Are You going to help the earth harvest the crops for food for the last three and one-half (3 ½) years?" Yahuah answered, "No! There is a patient waiting for Me as *HaMachiach* (the Messiah or Anointed) shown by those who keep God's commandments, who cleave to righteousness in spite of much temptation, and who refuse to pay homage to the god of this world, Satan, because firm in the faith that I, Yahusha Yahuah, am King. Physical science, linguistic knowledge, and political wisdom, will be antiquated. Those persecuted by the beast, will rest from persecutions. The "crown" is the crown of victory; the hour of conquest is at hand. The sickle shows that the harvest has come. Do you understand now the meaning of this part of the vision Polycarp?" Youthful Polycarp nodded his head in affirmation and said, "Yes, Master."

Yowchanan pleaded, "Silence, I can see more!" Then he began, "*A different angel issued forth from out of the Temple, screaming out loud in a great voice to the One sitting on the cloud,* **'Dispatch Your gathering hook for harvesting and harvest because the hour for You to harvest has come because the crop was mature of the whole globe.'** *The One sitting on the cloud threw His gathering hook for harvesting on the whole globe and the crop of the globe was harvested.*"

Yahuah said, "Let Me elaborate so that there is not any misunderstanding. At this point in time the earth will be reaped so far as My children are concerned. The end has come; the entire church is redeemed to My side and made safe from the evil temptations of the earthly standards set up by Satan and his hierarchy. Also the work contemplated is accomplished; and the results of the work done in My Name are like a glorious harvest."

Yowchanan quickly added, "*A different angel issued forth from out* *of the Temple in Heaven, the eternal abode of Yahuah. He also possessed a rapid gathering hook for harvesting. A different angel issued forth from out of the altar possessing delegated influence over the fire and he spoke with a great scream to the one possessing the rapid gathering hook for harvesting relating in words, '**Dispatch your rapid gathering hook for harvesting and collect the vintage of the clusters of grapes of the coiling vine of the globe because its grapes are mature.** The angel threw his gathering hook for harvesting into the globe and collected the vintage of the coiling vine of the globe and threw the grapes into the great wine vat of the breathing hard passion of anger of Yahuah. The wine vat was trampled outside the city and came forth blood from out of the trough of the wine vat unto the bridles of the horses and one thousand and six hundred stadia (200 miles)."*

Yahuah Yahusha explained this part of the introduction to the last three and one-half (3 ½) years of the Tribulation Period, "The grapes mentioned here are 'wild grapes', the unbelieving who choose to follow and worship Satan, the anti-messiah and his beast. The blood represents all their evil sins that will be exposed and judged. The sixteen (4x4) hundred stadia (200 miles) represents a judgment complete and full, reaching to all four corners of the earth."

The Messiah addressed Yirmyah and youthful Polycarp saying, "Yowchanan grows very weary and exhausted. I must let him rest now before I can continue the vision of the last parts of the introduction to the Tribulation Period. Please hand Me your cloak Polycarp and Yirmyah get the blanket of Yowchanan." Polycarp handed his Master the cloak and Yahuah put it behind the head of aged Yowchanan and then Yahusha took the tattered blanket and covered the chilled body of Yowchanan. Yahuah gently touched the forehead of Yowchanan with His right index finger and simply said, "Rest, My trusted friend." The body of Yowchanan became surrounded by a great white light as it glowed in the dark and cold cave. The two companions in the cave marveled at the miracle with such awe that they did not notice that the presence of Yahuah Yahusha had disappeared. After a moment in time, the chill of the cave biting and gnawing on their bones brought them back to their natural senses as Polycarp ventured outside to fetch more firewood. Meanwhile Yirmyah stirred the remaining glowing red embers of the dying campfire and added the leftover small twigs to help reignite the soon to be blazing fire with dancing yellow and orange flames. After the span of about half an hour, Polycarp returned with an armful of wood to reignite the campfire to take the chill off the damp air of the musty cave.

The quiet whispering of the conversation between youthful Polycarp and Yirmyah (Jerry) so as not to awaken sleeping Yowchanan soon gave into silence as the mesmerizing and methodical dancing shadows of the blazing campfire filled the dirt walls of the otherwise dark cave. Then silence gave way to yawning and heavy eyelids as Yirmyah and Polycarp succumbed to their own weariness as they both laid down and fell fast asleep on the cool dirt floor of the cave.

While the three ministers of the Gospel of Yahusha Yahuah were fast asleep and living out some sort of drama in the land of dreamland, outside the cave in the spiritual realm it was growing dark and dreary. Unbeknownst to them, after Yahuah Yahusha put Yowchanan to sleep and departed, He sent His archangels Michael, Uriel, and Raphael to guard the cave and keep the three ministers safe from demonic harm. He knew that Satan would not want the next part of the introduction to the last part of the Tribulation Period to be revealed to mankind. Therefore, Satan not wasting an opportunity to stop the truth of Yahuah shrieked with all his might like a screaming black raven and sent out the great Vulture of death to kill the three ministers in the cave. Its large jagged black massive wings beat furiously the air of the smoky abyss as it rose towards earth with its putrid smell of death and decay. Joining the massive black beast with its long talons of poison were demonic giants Salagrund, Metadrone, and Ziggul.

Now, Salagrund was the demon master of disease looking like a black hairy-legged tarantula with red fangs and large transparent tear-dropped wings that propelled his massive body through the air. Metadrone was the demon master of destruction adorning the appearance of a horrific alligator covered with rows of shield-like iron scales and glowing green eyes. His wide mouth contained rows upon rows of razer-sharp teeth and his long powerful tail was like a battering ram. Finally, Ziggul was the demon master of deceit. His appearance was that of a gigantic lizard with a thin, narrow and long forked-tongue that constantly shot out of his black mouth dropping drops of acid like salvia. Thus death, disease, destruction and deceit sped through the darkness of the night towards the prison island of Patmos to the hollow and barbaric laughter of Satan full of hatred and malice.

The force of their horrific wings beating against the air produced gale-like winds on the island as the waves of the sea beat furiously against the shoreline and exploded against the rocks of the cliffs. The sound of their wings was a distant roar that became a deafening crescendo as they approached the cave entrance of the unsuspecting three ministers of the Gospel. As they were about to fly over the edge of the island, they were met by the warrior archangels who immediately engaged the demonic beasts in battle. Michael delivered a stunning blow to the gigantic Vulture of Death throwing the demonic bird-like creature into somersaults through the air. Salagrund wheeled around just in time to block a blow delivered by

Uriel and Metadrone squared off against Raphael who was attacking Ziggul with his acid producing tongue.

Michael hurried to the aide of Raphael who was fighting off both Metadrone and Ziggul. The long forked acid producing tongue of Ziggul repeatedly struck out against Michael but Michael was too quick for the cumbersome lizard. Michael grabbed the tail of the gigantic lizard and spun him around like a tornado in circles. Green bubbling acid rotated in the tornado like a whirlwind striking the grotesque creature's own body making it scream with intense pain leaving patches of bloodied skin all over his body. Finally, Michael let go of the tail sending Ziggul spinning into the agitated sea below entering into the frothing waters with a big splash. The demonic spirit of the loathsome creature instantly returned back to the dark abyss screaming with an eerie scream as the water swallowed him up. The Vulture of Death had regained his senses and returned to the battle to engage with Michael once more.

In the meantime Uriel was locked in a tight battle with Salagrund the demonic tarantula. Its eight long and hairy legs kept Uriel at a distance away from its body to prevent a fatal blow by the sword of Uriel. Uriel tried spinning around to get behind the massive black beast but the demonic creature was too nimble. Then Uriel faked a jab with his long sword and with his free hand threw a blinding ball of bright light towards the beady eyes of the horrific insect. The ball of light hit its intended mark, temporarily blinding the eyes of the mean-spirited spider giving Uriel a fraction of time to swoop below the soft underbelly of the demonic tarantula and thrust his long sword deep into the soft flesh of this Satanic beast. The body of the demonic tarantula crumpled into a heap as it fell helplessly against the rocky cliffs as its long red fangs scraped several boulders loose which crushed and covered the dreadful animal. With a bone-chilling scream its demonic spirit abandoned the lifeless body and headed back to the smoking abyss in utter defeat to face the wrath of its master Satan.

Uriel quickly headed to the side of Archangel Michael to help battle the massive black Vulture of Death while Raphael continued to do battle against Metadrone. The demonic alligator swung its massive battering ram like tail at Raphael trying to lure the archangel into its jaws of flesh-piercing death by its rows of razor sharp teeth. Raphael kept a safe distance from that crushing tail and when his sword would make contact with the body of the massive alligator sparks would fly as metal struck against the rows of iron like scales that protected the body of this demonic reptile. Archangel Raphael relentlessly maneuvered and struck out against this cold-blooded foe but to no avail.

Finally, Raphael made a strategic lateral move to attack the underside of the unprotected area of the bottom jaw of the scaly monster. However, just as Raphael began his dive the battering ram like tail of the alligator just grazed the corner of the shield of Raphael sending him off balance towards the edge of the rocky cliffs. Instantly, Metadrone spun its large body around in an attempt to catch Raphael in its piercing jaws of death. Raphael recovered his balance quickly and with natural instinct quickly thrust his long sword towards the underside of the bottom jaw as Metadrone tried to blind his vision with rays of blinding green light shooting from his glowing green eyes.

The reaction of Raphael had been too quick as the steel blade caught the throat of Metadrone the alligator monster of destruction. Its massive body fell like a huge bolder to the ground making a dull thud causing what seemed to be a small earthquake upon the prison island. The spirit of Metadrone whimpered as it left the now breathless body as it headed back to the smoke of the boiling cauldron of evil in defeat to its master Satan and his demonic minions. The massive black Vulture of Death saw that he was the only one remaining instantly gave up the conflict with Michael and Uriel. It headed back to the lair of Satan in total defeat regretting the torturous wrath of the dark lord.

The three ministers of the Gospel were safe as Michael, Uriel and Raphael returned to the throne of Yahuah. The gale-like winds ceased hammering the island as they became a gentle evening breeze. The dark clouds of the black smoke from the boiling cauldron of Satan had cleared and the evening sky was once again blanketed with countless glimmering stars. The minor shaking of the ground from the impact of the body of Metadrone only shook a few small rocks loose above the cave entrance where Yowchanan (John), Yirmyah (Jerry) and youthful Polycarp were finishing up their night's rest. Even the Roman sentinels standing guard in the garrison did not even notice the vibration.

In the very early dawn, Yirmyah was awakened by the noise of a few remaining loose rocks tumbling down the side of the hilly cliff where the cave was tucked away amongst its face. Yirmyah yawned and stretched both of his arms upwards straightening the kinks in his muscles from laying on the hard cold dirt floor of the damp and musty cave. He threw off his tattered blanket and slowly walked to the entrance of the cave. When he arrived at the entrance and looked out at the vast early dawn panoramic view and he noticed what seemed to be a tranquil and beautiful scene. In the east was a darkened sky with a rising sliver of brilliant yellow, light orange and royal purple peeking its way into the new day. The birds were singing their melodious songs of joy to Yahuah Yahusha praising Him for another episode in the life of a feathered creature. A very gentle breeze whisked effortlessly through the leaves of the bushes and trees causing the leaves to wave as if they were saying 'hello and good morning' with their light rustling sound.

Yirmyah stood there, in the entrance of the mouth of the cave being mesmerized by the beauty created by the finger of Yahuah Yahusha spoken into existence by the power of the Sacred Breath (Holy Spirit). The gentle colors of the brightening eastern skyline were accompanied by a symphony of rustling leaves and the distant sounds of the relaxing and peaceful beat of the rolling waves of the sea coming ashore and then returning back to the vast sea of water blending in with the chorus of melodious bright-colored feathered birds chirping their harmonizing songs. Yirmyah silently wondered why this morning was so different for other mornings exhibiting what seemed to be a new peace and fresh beginning. It was as if the new day was celebrating the triumphant victory of a treacherous battle.

The experience of the breathtaking moment of the magnificent and elaborate scene of the grandiose handiwork of Yahuah Yahusha was unwillingly interrupted by the sound of the trumpet call for the first hour of the day which signaled the changing of the watchtower guards for the Roman garrison. It also served as call for those who had to work in the salt mines and rock quarries to report to their respective work details or be severely flogged. However, Yowchanan and his two companions received a pardon from work detail because of his age and health conditions. When they arrived at Patmos for their *publica custodia* (incarceration) the *Dux,* the island overseer, decided that because of the physical condition of Yowchanan, (John) that *vincula publica* (wearing of chains) would kill Yowchanan too soon. Therefore, he sentenced them to die what he thought would be a slow death of malnutrition and exposure to the elements of the forsaken island living as scavengers.

Yirmyah went back inside the cold, musty and dark cave to wake up his sound sleeping companions. First he had to wake up rhythmic snoring youthful Polycarp who had to get the daily firewood and miniscule rations of rotten and spoiled food. Polycarp mumbled and grumbled as he set up yawning and scratching his youthful raggedy beard. Then he made his way to the entrance of the cave to start his daily trek. Yowchanan (John)…..

10

...was much easier and less moody to wake up than youthful Polycarp. This morning as was the case for every morning, Yirmyah (Jerry) and Yowchanan joined together in a quiet time of prayer and meditation upon the will of Yahuah Yahusha for their lives petitioning for physical strength and spiritual wisdom to accomplish the plan of Yahuah Yahusha for their lives. After a moment in time, youthful Polycarp returned with an armload of dry firewood and a small satchel that contained their daily meager food rations. He placed a few of the dry twigs upon the smoldering white embers and stirred them as some became red and ignited the twigs with dancing yellow and orange flames. After a breakfast of stale bread from the Roman garrison and cool water from the spring, Yirmyah shared his experience of the morning beauty of today's early dawn spectacular performance of creation.

Out of nowhere a deep and familiar voice like thunder announced, "*Shalom!*" The three companions quickly bowed their heads and responded, "*Shalom*, Master Yahuah." When they lifted their heads, they were surrounded by a surreal and warm white light that enveloped the entire cave. Yirmyah quickly gathered his quill pen and papyrus sheets because he knew that Yahuah Yahusha was present to continue the vision with Yowchanan. Then Yahusha said, "Today through Yowchanan I will continue to share with you the mystery of the introduction to the last three and one-half (3 ½) years of the Tribulation Period. In it I will describe the beast (anti-messiah) and his false prophet. Yowchanan look at the opposite wall and tell Me what you see!"

Yowchanan began to share saying, *"He stood on the sand of the sea, I see from out of the sea a dangerous animal coming up, having seven heads and ten hours with ten diadem crowns of royalty and on the heads of it were names of vilification against Yahuah. The dangerous animal which I saw was similar to a leopard and its feet in the manner of a ferocious bear and the mouth of it in the manner of a lion. The dragon serpent gave to it his power and his stately seat throne and great delegated influence."*

Yahuah Yahusha said, "Let Me explain the vision. Satan standing means that he will establish lordship on the earth. The sand represents the people and the seashore represents all the nations of the earth. The sea represents the demonic kingdom and the dangerous animal is the anti-messiah, known as the 'beast'. The seven heads are symbolic of a perfect (the number seven) governmental and religious system and the ten horns represent complete power handed over by the ten most powerful nations of the world. The ten crowns are symbolic of complete authority of the rulers of the ten nations. The leopard represents Nimrod of ancient Babylon who started the first organized religion against Yahuah. Its priests wore leopard or spotted skins and leopards were used for their hunting and cunning ability. The feet of a bear are symbolic of enormous power and the mouth of a lion is symbolic of rule and law is to be unwavering and to disagree will be fatal to those in opposition."

Yowchanan (John) continued, *"I see one of the heads as having been butchered to death and the wound of its death was healed. All the whole globe admired the dangerous animal. They prostrated themselves in homage doing reverence and adoration to the dragon serpent who gave delegated influence to the dangerous beast and they prostrated themselves in homage doing reverence and adoration to the dangerous animal relating in words,* **'Who is like the**

dangerous animal who is able to battle with it.' *Was given to its mouth speaking great things and vilifications against Yahuah. It was given delegated influence to act for forty-two months (3 ½ years)."*

Yahuah Yahusha stopped Yowchanan and said, "The head represents organized religion with its man-made theologies, false doctrines, self-serving worship traditions all which from the church pulpits teach lies replacing sacred truths. All religions of the world will come to an end when the anti-messiah establishes his lordship on the earth. Then organized worship will be re-established and brought back to life as beast worship of the anti-messiah. Of course the dragon serpent is Satan himself and the anti-messiah will only have the power of Satan during the last three and one-half (3 ½) years and it will be unrestrained. The anti-messiah will set all political and religious authority against Me." Then He said, "Yowchanan please continue with what you see."

So Yowchanan began once again with the vision, *"It opened up its mouth in vilification against Yahuah to vilify His name and His cloth tent hut tabernacle and those in Heaven residing in tents. It was given to make warfare with the sacred ones and to subdue them. It was given delegated influence over every tribal branch and language and race. All those living on the whole globe will prostate themselves in homage to do reverence and adoration to it, of whom was not written the name in the Scroll of Life of the Lamb having been butchered from the conception of the world. If anyone possesses an ear let him hear. If anyone convenes together captivity, he goes into captivity. If anyone will kill by a war knife it is necessary for him to be killed with a war knife. Here is the cheerful endurance and the moral conviction for the truth of Yahuah especially reliance upon the Anointed Messiah for salvation."*

Yahusha Yahuah explained, "During this time is an open and incited persecution against those church members who still remain on the earth. All those who worship the anti-messiah instead of Me will not be written in My Scroll of Life and will spend eternity in the torment of hell. I am the Lamb who was butchered on the cross at Calvary for the redemption of mankind and eternal forgiveness of their sins if they only believe and act upon My Gospel Message."

Then Yowchanan continued to speak as Yirmyah recorded, *"I can see a different dangerous animal coming up from out of the soil of the globe and had two horns, two similar to a lamb and spoke in the manner of a dragon serpent. All it did in front of its face was with the delegated influence of the first dangerous animal. It made the whole globe and those living in it that they should worship the first dangerous animal of which was healed its wound of death. It does great supernatural indications in order that it even makes fire to descend down from out of the sky onto the soil of the globe in front of the faces of human beings."*

Yowchanan paused while Yahusha explained its meaning, "The second dangerous animal is the False Prophet. The soil of the globe refers to the advancing of intelligence of the world, its increase in knowledge and wisdom and the wider world power which is worshipped. His power lies in deception as well as violence. His outward appearance is that of meekness and gentleness like a lamb but his thoughts are those of the dragon serpent Satan influencing mankind to have self-seeking adoration of pleasures, honors, occupations, and influences which spring from the earth such as the pursuit of powers which are worldly. His voice is exercised by the papacy and corrupted clergy. Even his miracles are tricks of deceit yet mankind will believe in him to worship the beast, the anti-messiah."

The sound of the voice of Yowchanan once again filled the illuminated cave saying, *"It causes those living on the globe to roam from the safety of truth because of the supernatural indications which were given it to do in front of the dangerous animal expressing in words to those living on the earth to make a likeness of the dangerous animal who has the wound of the war knife and lived. It was given to it a demonic spirit to the likeness of the dangerous animal in order that even the likeness of the dangerous animal could speak and might make as many as would not prostrate themselves in homage to do reverence and adoration to the likeness of the dangerous animal that they would be killed outright."*

Yahuah Yahusha explained further, "Mankind will refuse to worship Me because worldly desires become more plausible to their greedy appetites. The likeness of the beast does not mean that it is a physical idol image but rather like an idea or belief that is a carbon copy of the anti-messiah. It is not set up in order to pay greater honor to the anti-messiah, but that it is an alternative offered to mankind so that those who hesitate to pay direct allegiance to the anti-messiah might overcome their scruples and worship something which resembles him. They will deceive themselves as their consciences will persuade them that they will not be worshipping the anti-messiah. Thus the idea or belief gives an appearance of reality which a mere image idol could not possess. In those days it will be a death sentence for those who refuse to worship the anti-messiah and his worldly beliefs or refuse to follow the orders of the false prophet." Yahusha Yahuah commanded, "Yowchanan tell us more of what you see! Yirmyah and Polycarp pay very close attention!"

The voice of Yowchanan seemed to change as it became more firm and serious as he shared what he saw, *"It makes all, the small and the great and the abounding with wealth and the beggars and paupers and the freemen and the slaves, that it may give to them a stamp of servitude of an etched statue on their right hand or on their foreheads, even in order that they could go to the market to purchase or trade, barter or sell except he possessing the stamp of servitude of an etched statue or the name of the dangerous animal or the number of it. Here is wisdom. The one possessing intellect let him compute the number of the dangerous animal. It is the number for a human being. The number of it is six hundred and sixty-six (666)."*

Yahuah explained the mystery of the mark, "This seal or mark is spiritual against the faith and character of My Gospel message. This evil brand means the acquiescence in character and action to the principles of this tyrannical world-power of the anti-messiah. The right hand is the symbol of toil and social intercourse and comes into consideration "as the instrument for action". The forehead is the symbol of character confession. The number six hundred and sixty-six (666) is simply a man who sets himself up and leads mankind to believe that he is more powerful than I. Yahuah Yahusha said, now I want to show you what will happen to the religious system set up by Satan's Babylon in order to establish deity worship of the anti-messiah."

Yahuah requested, "Yowchanan continue to tell Yirmyah and Polycarp about the introduction to the last three and one half (3 ½) years of the Tribulation Period especially the religious system," Yowchanan obliged and said, *"One of the angels possessing the seven broad shallow cups came and spoke with me relating in words,* **'Come, I will show you the decision against the great strumpet whore sitting on the many waters, with whom the sovereigns of the whole globe indulged in the unlawful lust of the harlot wore and became intoxicated from her wine of harlotry, adultery and incest, those residing permanently on the whole globe.'** *He carried me away into a desert by the Breath (Spirit). I saw a crimson colored (red) woman sitting on the dangerous animal, full of names of vilification against Yahweh, possessing seven heads and ten horns. The woman was clothed in purple and scarlet (red) and being bespangled with golden ornaments and precious stones and pearls possessing a drinking vessel made of gold in her hand, full of detestable idolatry ad impurity of her harlotry, adultery and incest. On her forehead was written her name:*

SECRET MYSTERY, BABEL THE GREAT, THE MOTHER OF THE WHORING STRUMPETS AND OF THE DETERSTABLE IDOLATRIES OF THE WHOLE GLOBE. *I saw the woman being intoxicated from the blood of the sacred ones and from the blood of the martyrs of Yahusha. I was full of wonderment seeing her with a great boldness.*"

Yowchanan continued, "*The angel said to me,* **'Why did you wonder? I will tell you the secret mystery of the woman and of the dangerous animal supporting her, the one possessing seven heads and ten horns. The dangerous animal which you saw was and is not and is about to come up from out of the depthless infernal abyss and goes to ruin and loss. Those living on the earth will wonder of whom has not written the name on the Scroll of Life from the conception of the world, looking at the dangerous animal that it was a thing and is not and it is indeed. Here is the mind having wisdom. The seven heads are seven mountains where the woman sits on them and are seven sovereigns. The five fell and the one is and other is not yet to come and when he comes he must remain a little amount of time. The dangerous animal which was and is not even he is the eighth and it is of the seven and goes to ruin and loss. The ten horns which you saw are ten sovereigns who have not yet received a royalty, realm or rule but will receive delegated influence as sovereigns in one hour with the dangerous animal. These have one mind and the miraculous power and their delegated influence they will give up to the dangerous animal. These will make war with the Lamb and the Lamb will subdue them because He is the Master of masters and Sovereign of sovereigns and those with Him are the called and selected trustworthy ones.**"

Yowchanan further stated what the angel said, "*He said to me,* **'The waters which you saw where the strumpet whore sits, are peoples and throngs of rabble even races and tongues. The ten horns which you saw on the dangerous animal, these will hate the strumpet whore and** *will make her laid waste and nude and they will eat her flesh and will burn her down to the ground with fire. For Yahweh gave into their hearts of feelings and thoughts to do His resolve and to do one mind and to give their royalty, realm and rule to the dangerous animal until the utterance of Yahuah will be concluded to the end. The woman whom you saw is the great city possessing a royalty, realm and rule over the sovereigns of the whole globe."*

Then Yahusha Yahuah interjected, "Let me explain what Yowchanan just told you. The great harlot is the organized religious system and the beast is the anti-messiah. The many waters is the entire earth including nonbelievers and those who profess to worship Me but support, align themselves and worship false gods. This false religious system will reject My Gospel, the power of Yahuah-like living and even the basic truths of My teachings. This organized religion will enter into a partnership with the powers and philosophy of Satan, represented by the world systems and its perceived immorality. Religious and political powers will be combined to unite and take spiritual control over all the nations of the earth."

Yahuah continued, "The leaders of the new organized religion will persecute My true believers and will become the melting pot for many different faiths, occults, creeds of which doctrine will not be of primary importance. The chief concern for this new organized religious system will be fellowship and unity with the system itself, its values and goals and will become a home for demons and a haunt for every evil spirit. The true kinship of this religious system is not with Me as the Messiah but with the world. Hypocrites and false prophets will achieve worldly success as a result of her doctrine, for she encourages worldly people to join her. She will also for a short time allow her members to profess Me as their God yet at the same time partake or commit adultery by practicing worldly manmade celebrations and practices. The coming religious system will be quick to compromise with political power and toleration of unrighteousness will be her trademarks. As a prostitute the apostate will sell her favor to the world at every opportunity."

Yahuah Yahusha added, "The scarlet beast is the world government of the anti-messiah which supports and promotes the religious system of the apostate spiritual power. The golden cup is symbolic of the churches in the world which appear to be beautiful on the outside but inside will be full of 'abominable things'. This will be the true spiritual condition of the apostate church during this time. The church that holds the golden cup will offer mankind both Me and worldly satisfaction. This will be a perverted gospel that will assure its members they can enjoy immorality and evil while at the same time My grace and mercy will make them accepted by Me as they practice their adultery of whoredom."

Yahusha Yahuah went on further, "The seven heads, seven mountains and seven kings are all in one the same. They are the worldly powers and nationalistic governments that support the anti-messiah. The eight is the coming kingdom of the anti-messiah who is currently at work even this present day of age as he will head up the final world empire. He belongs to the same ungodly worldly system as the first seven. The ten horns and ten kings are nations that will have great political power and support the future world order of the anti-messiah. They make up a world confederacy of nations that will greatly oppose Me and My true Gospel of salvation."

The majestic voice of Yahuah Yahusha continued to fill the inside of the walls of the cave saying with encouragement, "My loyal companions do not be afraid of these visions that I am sharing through My cousin Yowchanan. They not only serve as a forthcoming of the final days on the earth but as an encouragement to My children that

We shall have the final victory over Satan and his unrighteousness. That is why I am explaining in detail through an introduction to the final three and one-half (3 ½) years of the Tribulation Period so that you will understand the events that will take place and not become overwhelmed as I actually share the final last forty-two months (3 ½ years) of the Tribulation Period with you."

The natural inquisitiveness of youthful Polycarp prompted him to ask, "So Master Yahusha, when are these events to take place? Will the end of the world be very soon?" Yahuah Yahusha responded, "It is not yours to know the hour that they will take place but to have the knowledge of the events so you will understand when the events that Yowchanan has described happen, My children will have the wisdom and foresight of what will take place without the fear of the unknown. You must take nourishment now before I go any further with the introduction. However, what I will tell you is that I have one more part to share with you and then the introduction will be completed. Now Polycarp go to the entrance of the cave and retrieve the blessing that I have provided for you and your companions."

When Yahuah Yahusha had finished speaking, the cold cave once again became silent and the bright presence of Yahuah vanished as the only light that transpired now was that of the small campfire. When Polycarp exited the mouth of the cave, his jaw dropped in astonishment because right before his eyes was,,,,

11

...a brown woven basket with a white linen cloth draped over the top of it sat under the bush to the right of the cave entrance. Youthful Polycarp extended both of his arms skyward and exclaimed, "*Todah, Melek Yahuah Yahusha* (Thank you, King Yahuah Yahusha)." He picked up the brown wicker woven basket and carried it inside the musty cave smiling from ear to ear. Yowchanan and Yirmyah clapped their hands together as Polycarp sat the basket down on the dirt floor of the cave and spread out the white linen cloth. With the affirmative nod of the head of Yowchanan, youthful Polycarp began to unload the basket of its delicious contents and set them on the white linen cloth.

First out of the basket was a warm golden-brown twisted loaf of *challah* bread followed by three large clusters of sweet purple seedless grapes. Next out of the woven basket was a clay platter heaped with smoked fish piping hot followed by a bowl of hummus. The final items to exit the much welcomed container was a carafe of unfermented grape juice and a small platter of the sticky honey morsel of *baklava* for dessert. After a joyous prayer of thanksgiving by Yowchanan (John), the three companions filled their hollow stomachs with the provisions of love that Yahuah Yahusha had provided for them.

After consuming the delicious morsels that were in the brown woven basket, the three companions were engaged in small talk in the early afternoon when instantly Yahuah Yahusha was seated between Yowchanan and Yirmyah. Yahusha said, "Now let Me show you the commercial aspect of Babylon and the destruction of the great city caused by My bowl judgments at the very end of the Tribulation Period." Yirmyah quickly scrambled to ready his quill pen and pampas grass paper and youthful Polycarp put the white linen cloth and pottery containers in the woven basket. Yahusha said, "Yowchanan look into My eyes and tell Me what you see."

Yowchanan began, *"After these things I saw a different angel descending down from out of Heaven, the eternal abode of Yahuah, possessing great privilege of delegated influence and the whole globe was brightened up from his glory. He exclaimed in a great voice with forcefulness relating in words,* **'Fallen, Babel the great has fallen and has become a dwelling place of demons, and a guarded place of every demonic spirit and a guarded place of every impure bird and being hated, because of the wine of the breathing hard passion of anger of her harlotry, adultery and incest which all the races have drunk and the sovereigns of the earth have indulged in her unlawful lustful acts of a harlot and the wholesale tradesmen of the whole globe from the power of her luxury became wealthy.'**

Yowchanan continued, *"I heard another voice from out of Heaven, the eternal abode of Yahuah relating in words,* **'Come out of her My people in order that you will not share in the company with her sins and that you will not receive of her wounding calamities. Because her sins joined together up to heaven, the eternal abode of Yahuah, and Yahuah remembered her wrong doings. Give back to her as also she had given back to you and render two-fold to her two-fold according to her works. In the drinking vessel in which she mixed her two-fold mix. By what things she rendered herself glorious and was luxurious by so much give to her torture and grief. Because in her heart of feelings and thoughts she says, 'I sit as a queen and I am not a widow and I do not see at all grief.' Therefore, in one day will come her calamities, death and grief and a scarcity of food and with fire she will be burnt down to the** *ground and consumed wholly because forceful is the Anointed Messiah Yahuah trying, condemning and punishing her.'*

The voice continued through Yowchanan, *'The sovereigns of the whole world will sob and wail loudly for her and will beat their breasts in grief over her, those having indulged in unlawful lustfulness of harlotry and having enjoyed the luxuries with her, when they see the smoke of her ignition as a great smelting, standing a great distance because of the fear of her torture relating in words, Woe, Woe for the great city, Babel the forcible city for in one hour came your justice of divine law. The wholesale tradesmen of the whole globe sobbed and wailed out loud and grieved over her because their cargo of wares no one goes to the market to purchase no longer, cargo wares of gold and of silver and of precious stones and of pearls and of fine white linen and of purple and of silk and of crimson-colored (red) and all wood from the fragrant citron tree and every container of ivory and every container of very precious and valuable wood and of copper and of iron and of glistening and sparkling marble, and cinnamon and aromatic powdered incenses and perfumed oil with myrrh and frankincense and wine and olive oil and fine wheat flour and wheat and domesticated animals, and sheep and horses and chariots and sound bodies of lives of human beings and the ripe plucked fruits of the longing for what is forbidden of your breath of sprit departed from you and all the fat things and radiant things departed from you and no longer not at all will you find them.'*

Yowchanan continued to repeat what he heard, *'These wholesale tradesmen, those becoming wealthy from her will stand at a great distance because of the fear of her torture sobbing and wailing out loud and grieving and relating in words, "Woe! Woe the great city having been clothed in linen and purple and crimson red and having been bespangled with golden ornaments and precious valuable stones and pearls. Because in one hour such great wealth was laid waste. Every captain and all the group on the sailing vessels, and boatmen and as many was work the sea stood from a far distance and shrieked and screamed like croaking ravens seeing the smoke of her ignition of smelting relating in words, what is similar to this great city? They threw rubbish and loose dirt on their heads and screamed sobbing and wailing out loud and grieving relating in words, woe, woe, for the great city by which all those possessing sailing vessels in the sea from her magnificent expansiveness because in one hour she was laid waste.'*

Yowchanan concluded the vision of the introduction of the final three and one-half years (3 ½) of the Tribulation Period by what he saw and heard, **'Rejoice over her oh Heaven, the eternal abode of Yahuah and the sacred ambassadors of the Gospel being official commissioners of the Anointed Messiah and the inspired prophets because Yahuah tried, condemned and punished your decision of crime upon her.'** *The one forceful angel lifted up a stone in the manner of a great grinding stone and threw it into the sea relating in words,* **'Thus on an attack Babel the great city will be thrown and yet will not be found at all. The sounds of harpists and of musicians and flute players and of trumpet players will not at all be heard in you any longer and every artisan of every art will not at all be found in you any longer. The sound of a grinding mill will not be heard in you any longer. The light of a lamp will not at all shine in you anymore. The voice of a groom and bride will not at all be heard in you any longer. For your wholesale tradesmen were the great ones of the whole globe for by your medication magic all the races were caused to roam from the safety of truth, and in her the blood of the inspired prophets and sacred ones was found and of all those having been killed of the whole globe."**

When Yowchanan had finished, Yahusha Yahuah said, "Now let me explain. The commercial system of the new world order is completely destroyed during this time. The reference is not solely that earthly merchandise is destroyed, but also to spiritual wares such as indulgences, idolatries, superstitions, worldly compromises. You see the apostate Church will make merchandise of men. At this time, My people are called out of the city Babylon because if they were to remain on earth, they would participate in its worldly sins of idolatry and experience its coming plagues of My bowl judgements following the seventh trumpet blast."

Yahusha continued the explanation, "The suffering and misery to fall on commercial Babylon will be in proportion to the self-glorifying and luxurious lifestyle she lived. The rich, powerful and unscrupulous enterprisers who rejected Me and piled up wealth to the injury of others will be stripped of their wealth in one day. Even the unfaithful Church whose principle will be *'Populus vult decipi, et decipiatur.'* (The people like to be deceived, and let them be deceived.) will be severely punished. The kings represent all those whose main concern is money, luxury, and gratification of pleasures will weep and mourn for the god of their life is destroyed. They can no longer profit in merchandise since their great riches are gone. I am clearly indicating My hatred for businesses and governments founded on greed and repressive power. I stand against individuals who seek riches, status and pleasure instead of the humble values that I present in My Gospel. Those who live in selfish luxury and pleasure will be brought down by My wrath!"

Yahuah Yahusha rendered the meaning, "I used the term 'one hour' which is symbolic of meaning in just a short time. The covetous and the worldly mourn; their minds were set upon a material glory, which has slipped away from their grasp. All saintly souls, whose affections have been towards righteousness and Me as the righteous King, can rejoice; for the wealth of holiness is imperishable. The great Babylon will be destroyed with great violence. The giant millstone thrown into the sea represents the fall of the political system that was set up. No music, no worker, no machinery, no light, no happiness shall be found in the city of Babylon any more as it has failed and became desolate. First, the religious system failed, then the commercial system and the final system to be destroyed is the one-world order political system. This now concludes the introduction to the final three and one-half (3 ½) years of the Tribulation Period. Just as a reminder as the fifth trumpet had sounded ending the first three and one-half years of the Tribulation Period, the anti-messiah has firmly established himself as the only savior of the world."

Yahuah then stated, "Now the second three and one-half years of the Tribulation Period will begin with the sounding of the sixth trumpet. Everything that I covered in the introduction of the final three and one-half (3 ½) years of the Tribulation Period will quickly take place. Yowchanan what do you see?"

Yowchanan began, *"The sixth angel sounded a blast of the trumpet. I heard a voice one from out of the four horns of the altar made of gold in front of the face of Yahuah, saying to the sixth angel who possessed the trumpet,* **'Loosen the four angels, those having been bound at the great River Euphrates (in Iraq).'** *The four angels were loosed, those having been prepared for that hour and day and month and year in order that they should kill the third part of human beings. The number of the body of troops of the cavalry force was two myriads of myriads (200 million). I heard the number of them."*

Yahuah Yahusha explained, "Do not become confused by the imagery but rather listen to its meaning. A horn symbolizes authority therefore the four horns represent My authority over the four corners of the earth, north, south, east and west. Also, the four angels represent one messenger angel who will punish mankind in all four directions of the earth. The Euphrates River is known historically for its natural boundary and a source for where hostile hosts arise. The river portrays the spiritual evils which afflict the ungodly in this life, and which give them, as it were, a foretaste of their doom in the life to come. The immense host of two hundred million (200,000,000) will have prolific powers of retribution because the harvest of unforgiven sin is misery."

Then Yowchanan continued with the vision of the sixth trumpet, *"In this way, I saw the horses as I gazed at the inspired appearance and those sitting on them, having flaming chest plates and a bluish-red color being almost black and yellow the color of sulfur. The heads of the horses in the manner of lions and out of their mouths is discharged fire and smoke and flashing sulfur burning with blue flames and smelling like rotten eggs. By these there were killed the third part of human beings from the fire and from the smoke and from the sulfur discharged from their mouths. For their delegated influence is in their mouths and in their tails for their tails are similar to sly and cunning snakes with sharp vision possessing heads and they do wrong with them."*

Yahusha made clear the symbolism, "The horses represent swiftness of action and their breastplates represent My perfect morality. Having the heads of lions represent great power. The three plagues symbolize sulfurous lust, the smoke of false doctrines, and the fires of wars. Their tails are masses of foot soldiers in which some of them will hide for ambush. Yowchanan what else do you see?"

Yowchanan responded, *"The remaining human beings who were not killed by these strokes of calamity causing wounds did not think differently to reconsider to feel moral compunction of the works of their hands in order that they will not prostrate themselves in homage doing reverence and adoration to demonic beings and images of heathen gods of gold and silver and bronze and stone and wood who are not able to see nor able to hear nor to tread all around or walk at large. They did not think differently to reconsider to feel* moral compunction of their murders nor of their medication magic nor of their harlotry, adultery and incest nor of their stealing."

Yahusha Yahuah gave a great sigh and then stated, "The purpose of the plagues of the sixth trumpet is designed to bring about repentance from mankind on the earth who are all lost following the worldly ways of Satan's demonic lies. It saddens My heart however that even after one third (1/3) of the unbelieving mankind remaining on earth is killed their hearts remain hardened and they continue to be deceived by the demonic self-serving lies of Satan. The remaining mankind refuses to repent from their worldly lusts such as greed, social status, Spiritism, occult, magic, demon worship, murder, violence, drugs, witchcraft, love of money, sexual immorality, homosexuality, theft, lawlessness and pornography. Yowchanan used the correct Greek word describing 'medication magic' as I have shown him *'pharmakia'* for sorcery. Yirmyah and young Polycarp you are well aware that sorcery is nothing but satanic witchcraft that is involved with the use of drugs. That is the very reason the medicine bag of a physician is called a 'pharmacy'! Now listen to Yowchanan carefully of the events that will take place next."

Aged Yowchanan (John), the beloved cousin of Yahusha Yahuah HaMachiach (the Anointed/Messiah) began slowly, *"I see a different strong angel descending down from out of Heaven, the eternal abode of Yahuah, having been clothed with a cloud and a rainbow on the head, his face as the sun and his feet in the manner of support posts of fire like lightning and he possessed in his hand a booklet having been opened up. He placed his right foot on the sea and the left on the soil of the globe, and exclaimed with a great voice in the manner that a lion roars. When he exclaimed, the voices of the seven roaring thunders themselves spoke. When the voices of the seven roaring thunders themselves spoke, I was about to write. I heard a voice from out of Heaven, the eternal\ abode of Yahuah relating in words to me,* **'Seal**

what things spoken by the seven roaring thunders and do not write those things."

As Yowchanan paused, Yahuah Yahusha began to explain what was just seen, "The strong angel is the Angel of Time. Being clothed with a cloud means that he is encompassed with a cloud, or enveloped in a cloud. This is a symbol of majesty and glory, and is represented as being accompanied with My divine presence. A rainbow upon his head is properly an emblem of peace. The symbol means that the angel came not for wrath, but for purposes of peace. A lovely token of My divine favor, and a symbol of My covenant and mercy toward penitent sinners. 'His face was as it were the sun' represents all the righteous that shall shine forth just as the sun and is an emblem of the light of My Gospel about to be diffused at this time in the darkness of worldly lusts. 'His feet as pillars of fire' signifies the steadiness and efficacy of his actions. His actions will be bright and shining as flame of lightning meaning that the faithful during this period of time will suffer persecution, and yet be preserved from the rage of their enemies."

Yahuah Yahusha continued, "To show the extent of his power and commission, this angel set his right foot on the sea toward the west, his left on the land toward the east, so that he looked southward. The sea of the west and the land of the east being under his feet is symbolic that the entire earth and mankind will need to be under submission to him as My messenger. His voice is the voice of courage and strength derived from Myself who is the 'Lion of the tribe of Judah.' However, to those who choose to be My enemies the roaring is an image of terror. The number seven is symbolic of perfection and the thunder is My voice of the Sacred Breath (Holy Spirit). Yowchanan was commanded by Me to seal up and not reveal what I had said to him so that the godly are thus kept from morbid ponderings over the evil to come, and the ungodly are not driven by despair into utter recklessness of life."

Then Yowchanan began with the vision once again, *"The angel whom I saw standing on the sea and on the land lifted up his hand to Heaven, the eternal abode of Yahuah and declared an oath by Him living to the ages of the Messianic Period, Who fabricated in original form the sky and the things in it and the soil of the whole globe and the things in it and the sea and the things in it,* **'There will no longer be time! But in the days of the voice of the seventh angel, whenever he is about to sound a blast of the trumpet even the secret mystery of Yahuah may end and be completed, as He preached to His slaves, the inspired prophets."**

Yahusha stopped Yowchanan from going further with the vision and began to explain, "My brothers and My beloved children listen closely. The Angel of Time is holding the book in his left hand and raises his right hand to Me as swearing an oath with Myself as a Witness of Truth. I am recognized as the Creator of all things on the land and the sea. The Angel of Time expresses that the time of the world is over and will come to a quick end when the seventh trumpet is sounded. It will usher in the bowl judgments of My wrath to be poured out upon the unbelievers of the world. Following the bowl judgments the Tribulation Period will come to a screeching halt and will usher in My Second Coming as the Great *HaMachiach* (the Anointed/Messiah) to reign during the Messianic Period of one thousand (1,000) years. I must show you what will happen next because...."

12

....Then all of a sudden, in an instant the voice of Yahusha Yahuah was silent and gone from their midst. What was so important that He had to tell them and why did He depart so suddenly? Even aged Yowchanan sat there in silence and a state of wondering. After a prolonged moment in time, youthful Polycarp asked, "Yowchanan what just happened and why was the vision stopped if Yahusha said we must know what will happen next?" Yowchanan answered softly, "Brother Polycarp I do not know, but it is not ours to question why and what our Master and our Yahuah does! He always reveals things in His timing and for His purpose!' Yirmyah nodded his head in agreement with Yowchanan and said, "*Ken, ken* (Yes, yes)."

The late afternoon was beginning to wane as a new evening was announcing its approaching arrival with a beautiful sunset in the western horizon. The sky was flawlessly painted with pastel pinks and purples supported underneath with brilliant yellows which blended in majestically with an array of oranges and reds which hugged and surrounded the sitting sun as it lowered itself behind the landscape of the earth. Even though the scene outside the dingy cave was a portrait of beauty, peace and tranquility, inside the walls of dirt and rock of the cave the spirit of youthful Polycarp remained unsettled and anxious.

Even though the young apprentice had not received any nourishment the entire day, the usual ravenous appetite of his belly was non-existent. In addition, his usual non-stop verbal assault of questions, teasing and jokes had disappeared. As Yowchanan and Yirmyah sat by the fire eating their ration of small morsels of stale bread and spoiled fruit, they tried to encourage and lift the spirit of youthful Polycarp. However, it was to no avail as Polycarp just sat there stoic in complete silence drowning in self-imposed apathy and apprehension. After Yowchanan (John) and Yirmyah (Jerry) had finished eating, they covered themselves with their tattered and worn-out blankets leaving youthful Polycarp sitting by the campfire staring into its dancing flames as he slowly poked at the red embers with a small twig. The two companions of Polycarp were soon fast asleep, yet he continued to drift and travel deeper into the silent world of puzzlement and deep thought.

No matter how hard Polycarp fought the urge, the rhythmic popping of the glowing red embers and the sound of the gentle breeze outside the cave entrance weighed heavy upon the eyelids of the youthful minister of the Gospel. After a small period of time, youthful Polycarp laid down beside the fire and fell asleep journeying down the peaceful paths of dreamland. His annoying and expected famous snoring and snorting soon filled the air of the darkened cave like the sounds of a harmonious symphony would fill the open air of an amphitheater.

In the very early morning hours long before the new sun could announce its coming arrival with a beautiful painted sunrise across the vast darkened eastern skies, the sleep of Yirmyah (Jerry) was stirred as he felt a strong presence of something in the midst of the three sleeping companions. His ears picked up the sounds of the intruder rustling through their belongings where the food supplies were usually kept. He slowly opened up his eyes and looked in that direction and saw the shadow of an unfamiliar bearded figure putting its face into their empty clay bowls. Then he quickly sat up grabbing his walking stick and yelling for Yowchanan to be awakened. Startled

Yowchanan opened his eyes and quickly grabbed the nearest object where he was sleeping for protection against the thief.

Youthful Polycarp remained asleep oblivious to the eminent danger that the intruder imposed upon their well-being. The long-bearded male with no clothes and shaggy hair covering his entire body looked up from his scavenging activities towards the two startled ministers of the Gospel. Yirmyah and Yowchanan slowly got up and cautiously surrounded and approached the intruder with their so called weapons ready to strike if needed. The intruder shook his head at them in defiance and charged at them in attack. However just as the thief was jumping over the sleeping body of youthful Polycarp, Polycarp was awakened by all the commotion and sat up colliding with the unwelcome intruder. The two collided sending both of them crashing off balance to the dirt floor of the cave. Then the eighty-seven year old Yowchanan (John) and the sixty-six year old Yirmyah (Jerry) seized the moment along with their stunned companion youthful Polycarp surrounded and chased the white shaggy male mountain goat out the cave entrance.

Yirmyah grabbed the right arm of Yowchanan and Polycarp secured the left arm as they helped the aged eighty-seven year old back inside the cave. The three companions, arm-in-arm began to laugh at the sight they must have been chasing that outnumbered animal out of the cave. As they neared the center of the cave, they recognized another visitor and instantly fell to their knees and exclaimed, "Master Yahuah!" Yahuah Yahusha responded, "Get up My brothers and come sit beside Me." They obeyed His instructions but He prevented youthful Polycarp from sitting down as He said, "Polycarp go to the Roman garrison just as it is your daily routine and get your daily rations. We shall wait for you to return and then eat breakfast before we continue with My vision to Yowchanan."

Polycarp did as his Master instructed and picked up the empty dirt-smudged sack and headed to the Roman garrison.

The fist rays of light were just beginning to shine in the eastern horizon and the morning trumpets were just sounding as he was approaching the large wooden gates of the compound. He got in line and held open the mouth of the dirt-smudged sack as the Roman soldiers threw in a few morsels of stale bread and rotten fruit. Then one of the soldiers remarked, "Well, well if it isn't the yapping puppy of the old dog up in the hills." This remark caused the other soldiers to begin laughing and barking in order to ridicule the young minister of the Gospel. Then the Roman soldier handing out the bread continued to chide Polycarp, "We missed you yesterday. What was the matter? Did the old dog not want his bone? How is the old hound anyway?" Polycarp replied, "Yowchanan is as fine as can be expected. Bless you for our daily rations." Then the Roman commander ordered, "Stop that man!" Two soldiers in battle gear grabbed youthful Polycarp and briskly escorted him to the commander. The Roman commander pointed his dagger at Polycarp and commanded, "Open the mouth of your sack puppy!" Polycarp did as commanded and then the Roman prison commander threw in another hard and stale biscuit." Then the commander said, "Give this to the old dog and maybe he will live another day in his dog house!" They released Polycarp and he hustled back to the cave as fast as his feet would carry him.

When he arrived back inside the cave huffing and puffing attempting to catch his breath, Yahusha asked, "Is something the matter Polycarp? Are you being chased by that goat again?" This brought a few chuckles from Yirmyah and Yowchanan as Polycarp replied, "No Master, the Roman soldiers were cruel with their words and I was afraid." Yahusha Yahuah said with comfort, "I am with you. What they intended for harm and evil, I will turn into good! Now hand me that extra biscuit the commander threw into your sack." Polycarp opened the mouth of the soiled sack with an astonished look on his face as he questioned, "But how did You...." Yahusha interrupted, "I AM, that I AM. The Ever Existent ONE!" Then Yahuah took the hard stale biscuit and covered it with His other hand. When He removed His covering hand, the small hard and stale biscuit had transformed into a large half loaf of *challah* bread. Also the small withered bunches of grapes that were in the sack were now large clusters of mouth-watering fresh red grapes.

The four sat around the fire and enjoyed their breakfast when Yahuah said, "Yirmyah get your quill and parchment and Yowchanan look into the fire and share with us what you can see." Yowchanan began, *"The voice which I heard from out of Heaven, the eternal abode of Yahuah, once more spoke with me relating in words,* **'Go, take the booklet, having been opened in the hand of the angel standing on the sea and on the soil of the whole globe.'** *I departed towards the angel relating in words to him,* **'Give me the booklet.'** *He expressed to me,* **'Take and devour it completely down and it will embitter your abdomen cavity but in your mouth it will be sweet in the manner of honey.'** *I took the booklet out of the hand of the angel and devoured it down, It was in my mouth in the manner of honey, sweet. When I ate it my abdomen cavity was made bitter. He related in words to me,* **"It is necessary once more for you to speak under inspiration and exercise the prophetic office in front of peoples and races and languages and many sovereigns."**

Yahuah Yahusha explained, "The open book signifies that its contents are not to be kept secret like those of the seven thunders. It is to be revealed for instruction, direction, encouragement and even a warning to mankind. It being bitter and sweet means that My Word is both a blessing and a curse. It is sweet to hear and blessings are sweet only through obedience savoring in the mouth to share with others. However when swallowed due to selfish greed and mixed with the digestive acids of worldly sin it becomes bitter with the judgement of sin."

Youthful Polycarp quickly questioned, "Wait a minute! Master Yahuah the angel said that Yowchanan was once again to preach. That means that he and we will not die here on this forsaken island." Yahusha answered, "Young Polycarp your intuition is correct. Just as My presence disappeared instantly last night, so shall be your remaining days on this island be! I warn you do not let the thoughts of going home distract you but focus on the task at hand now which is to finish revealing the mystery of My vision of Revelation to Yowchanan."

Then Yowchanan once more revealed more of the vision, *"Was given to me a reed similar to a cane and the angel stood relating in words,* **'Rouse up from your lying in inactivity and measure the size of the Temple of Yahuah, and the altar and those prostrating themselves in homage and in reverence and adoration in it. The outside of the Temple open to the wind ejected outside do not measure the size of it for this reason it was given to the foreign pagan races and they will trample the sacred city for forty -two months (3 ½) years. I will give to My two witnesses and they will speak under inspiration and exercise the prophetic office having been clothed in mohair for one thousand and two hundred and sixty days (1,260=3 ½ years)"**

"These are the two olive trees and the two lamp stands of the globe standing in front of the face of Yahweh. If anyone chooses to harm them, fire is discharged from out of their mouths and devours their hating adversaries and if anyone wishes to do wrong to them in this way it is necessary for him to be killed. These possess the delegated influence to close the sky in order that it does not moisten with a shower of rain in their days of prophecy predictions and they possess delegated influence over the waters, to turn them to blood and to smite the whole globe with every wounding calamity as if they wish'

'Whenever they complete and end their judicial evidence given, the dangerous animal will go up from out of the depthless and infernal abyss and will make war with them and will subdue them and will kill them. Their bodies will exist on the wide open square of the great city which is divinely called Cdom (Sodom) and Mitsrayim (Egypt) where indeed our Anointed Messiah was impaled on the cross. Some will see from the peoples and tribal branches and languages and races their bodies for three and a half days (3 ½). Their bodies they did not allow to be placed in burial places. Those living on the globe will be happy and cheerful over them and will rejoice. They will dispatch presents to one another because those two inspired prophets tortured those living on the globe."

"After three and a half days, a current of air, the Breath of Life from out of Yahuah entered into them and they stood up on their feet and great fear fell on those being spectators of them. They heard a great voice from out of Heaven, the eternal abode of Yahuah, relating in words to them, 'Come up here.' Then they went up in the cloud into Heaven, the eternal abode of Yahuah. In that hour came into being a great earthquake of the ground and the tenth part of the city fell and the names of human beings that were killed in the earthquake of the ground were seven thousand (7,000) and the remaining ones became alarmed with fear and gave glory to Yahuah of Heaven, the eternal abode of Yahuah. The second woe of grief departed. Lo, the third woe of grief is coming suddenly and without delay."

As soon as Yowchanan had finished with what he saw and heard, Yahuah began to explain the vision, "The measuring of the Temple represents measuring the spiritual condition of mankind. Measuring itself implies protecting from impending dangers of those who are My followers. Those in the outer court are those who worship in a false manner with dissembling hearts and will be found among My enemies. My enemies will desecrate My Sacred City Yruwshalaim (Jerusalem) and tread under foot anything having to do with Me, My Gospel or My Church. The two olive trees will be a means of supplying grace to the church. Just as the olive tree furnishes oil for the lamps, these olive trees, which are my witnesses properly denote that they will be ministers of My Truth. The candlesticks then represent that the witnesses are My lamp-bearers."

Yahusha Yahuah continued explaining, "My lamp-bearers are armed with the spiritual might of My Word which when accepted and lived by brings about peace but when rejected causes pain and danger. Their words will be like burning coals and flames. The rain represents blessings which will not rain upon the followers of the anti-messiah. The term waters symbolizes people, multitudes, nations and tongues over whom the anti-messiah reigns. Turning the waters into blood refers to the confusions and wars raised among the people on the account of the prophesying of these witnesses who will be treated with indignity and contempt. The two witnesses being killed means that their preaching will be silenced for a period of time. The term Sodom refers to the wickedness of mankind and its great immorality. Whereas the term Egypt is given for the oppression and slavery caused by the worldliness of the anti-messiah. An earthquake is a symbol of commotion, agitation, and change of great political revolutions."

Yahuah finished by saying, "The second woe is past, thus the Tribulation Period is over and the third woe which is the judgments full of My wrath are about to rain upon the unbelieving people who remain on earth with the anti-messiah and his false prophet. Just before the seventh trumpet sounds all My followers will be gathered unto Me for protection from My wrath of judgement against the unbelievers on the earth. And then...."

"Unseen Footsteps of Jesus"
OLAM
HABA
(Future World)
Mysteries Book 1- "Pre-Dawning"
Jerry Ayers

"Unseen Footsteps of Jesus"
OLAM
HABA
(Future World)
Mysteries Book 2- "The Dawning"
Jerry Ayers

"Unseen Footsteps of Jesus"
OLAM
HABA
(Future World)
Jerry Ayers

"Unseen Footsteps of Jesus"
OLAM
HABA
(Future World)
Jerry Ayers

"Unseen Footsteps of Jesus"
OLAM
HABA
Jerry Ayers

"Unseen Footsteps of Jesus"
OLAM
HABA
(Future World)
Jerry Ayers

"Unseen Footsteps of Jesus"
OLAM
(Future World)
Mysteries Book 7- "The Sunset"
Jerry Ayers

Future World
Jerry Ayers